50 JAPANESE SHORT STORIES
FOR BEGINNERS

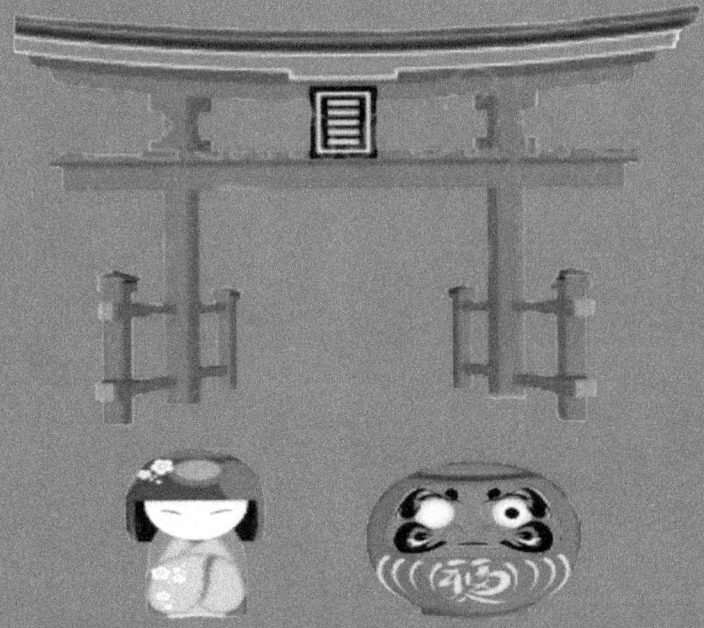

Read Entertaining Japanese Stories
to Improve Your Vocabulary and Learn Japanese While Having Fun

Yokahama English Japanese Language and Teachers Club

50 JAPANESE SHORT STORIES FOR BEGINNERS

Read Entertaining Japanese Stories to Improve your Vocabulary and Learn Japanese While Having Fun

Japanese Edition III
Including Hiragana, Kanji, and Furigana

© Copyright 2020 by Yokahama English Japanese Language & Teachers Club

License Notice: This document is geared towards providing exact and reliable information in regards to the topic and issue covered. In no way is it legal to reproduce, duplicate, or transmit any part of this document in either electronic means or in printed format. Recording of this publication is strictly prohibited and any storage of this document is not allowed unless with written permission from the publisher.

All rights reserved: The information provided herein is stated to be truthful and consistent, in that any liability, in terms of inattention or otherwise, by any usage or abuse of any policies, processes, or directions contained within is the solitary and utter responsibility of the recipient reader. Under no circumstances will any legal responsibility or blame be held against the publisher for any reparation, damages, or monetary loss due to the information herein, either directly or indirectly. The information herein is offered for informational purposes solely, and is universal as so. The presentation of the information is without contract or any type of guarantee assurance.

Disclaimer: The author of this book is not liable for the actions of any reader of this book; all the information is of the author's personal opinion.

Table of Contents

Foreword 7

Introduction and A Short History of The Language 8

Discover One of The Most Fascinating Languages and Its Culture ... 9

Explaining the Language 11

Modern Japanese Culture and Language 12

Follow This Easy Reading Guide 14

Beware of Styles And Expressions 16

Before You Get Started 17

Part 1: Japanese Stories for Beginners Including Hiragana, Kanji And Furigana 18

Part 2 Japanese Short Stories for intermediate students including Hiragana, Kanji and Furigana 102

Foreword

Thank you for buying this book! It indicates that you are prepared to engage with Japanese in brand-new and different ways. You possibly might also have a taste for good short stories. Reading Japanese short stories is an excellent method of studying the language, it's far more convenient and interesting compared to the conventional path of drilling vocabulary, and struggling with grammar workouts at an out-of-date school. Instead, you will get a new approach that does not rely upon outdated learning strategies and endless repetitions. The technique of learning through reading stories will produce results in a short time and will give you cultural understanding along with language skills. If you are striving for more in terms of enhancing your language skills with this method you are on the right path! Reading a prepared short story book is a fun and easy way to learn a new language, however, there are a few other activities you can start to improve your language skills. Many students are searching for a native speaking educator or signing up in standard language courses. Of course, the best way to learn Japanese would be to spend extended time in Japan. However, there are cheaper options; some students like audio-learning or listening to Japanese radio programs, others are checking out interesting publications as well as traditional workbooks. This book contains entertaining stories written in Japanese, with a corresponding translation of each paragraph to the English language. We have included a variety of genres: travel, suspense and mystery, using true storytelling and fascinating aspects of daily life in Japan

Introduction and A Short History of The Language

Japanese is a sophisticated language and is different from European as well as American languages, so allow us to offer you a brief background and introduction of the Japanese language.

The earliest remaining Japanese texts date back to the eighth century AD. Its origins depend on the Altaic language family. The Japanese of this duration is referred to as Old Japanese. A distinct function of Old Japanese was that it had 8 vowels and did not differentiate between long and short vowels. Japanese has actually been affected by several languages. Perhaps the most substantial borrowing in Japanese has actually been done from Chinese. In the third or fourth century AD, most of Japan had adopted the Chinese writing. Therefore large parts of ancient Japanese can be traced back to the Chinese language system. Modern Japanese culture, as well as the Japanese language, is a mixture of various foreign and traditional influences.

There are three kinds of character types used in writing: Hiragana (a phonetic system); Katakana (a phonetic system used mostly for foreign words); and Kanji (unique symbols with their own meaning and adopted from the Chinese).

Discover One of The Most Fascinating Languages and Its Culture

The stories in this book are written in Hiragana, Katakana, and about 250 basic Kanji characters which correspond to the beginner and low intermediate levels. As mentioned before, we have also included paragraph-by-paragraph English translation, which will accelerate the learning process quite a bit.

A word about the so-called Kanji characters. Japanese consists of three different character sets. Some people say, "the Japanese language is difficult". One of the reasons might be the Kanji, however, the Kanji can be written in Kana characters.

In this book Kanji characters have Furigana. Furigana (振り仮名) is a Japanese reading aid and their translation to English is listed in vocabulary section after each story. As you can see, Japanese is indeed a challenging language, but while you advance with your skills you might be surprised to find out how many English words have been adopted and used as Katakana words. Sometimes they don't even sound like English anymore. For example (アップル) Apple, (テーブル)Table, (ウォーター)Water.

This book covers both the formal and the casual style used in the Japanese language, dialogues in both styles of masculine and feminine, abbreviations, and well-known Japanese onomatopoeia. In addition to expanding your Japanese vocabulary, by reading this book you will find that Japanese language and customs differ depending on gender, time, background, generations, social environment, and individual circumstances.

As you go through the dialogues, you may notice that spoken Japanese sometimes differs from what you have studied in ordinary textbooks. Spoken language often varies from the written language, and at first glance it can seem grammatically incorrect. For example, particles, subjects, objects, or even predicates can be omitted. Generally speaking, Japanese sentences tend to be vague. The actual words establish a conversation, but you often need to read between the lines.

Explaining the Language

In Japanese a word-for-word translation is not always possible. Many kinds of abbreviations and omission happen in English as well, however, it is more frequent in Japanese.

There are expressions such as 「阿吽(あうん)の呼吸(こきゅう)」or「つうと言(い)えばかあ」which mean "understanding silence".

In Japan, certain people, especially from traditional backgrounds don't even need speech to communicate.

"Silent conversations" and "mental connections" are another form of how Japanese are communicating.

Japanese language in general is a mixture of old and historical idioms and various foreign and traditional influences, especially Chinese. However, as mentioned earlier there are three kinds of character types used in writing: Hiragana, Katakana (a phonetic system used mostly for foreign words); and Kanji. Sometimes the cultural mixture can be noticed by observing the combination of the characters. For example:

(ごめんなさい) I'm sorry (アメリカ) America (世界) World (日本に住むアメリカ人)Americans who live in Japan.

Modern Japanese Culture and Language

The Japanese draw a clear border in between the "inside" and the "outside". Like in other Asian countries, the Japanese have a tendency to show "two faces". The household and "internal circle" represents the inside. With family and friends they talk "openly" in a candid style. At work or when they speak to strangers, Japanese speak in more formal styles, particularly to individuals that belong outside their "intimate circle". But then again only to "insiders" they may show their true colors, when they are not under some sort of pressure, once they feel secure in their inner "circle" of family and friends. Once the ice is broken, Japanese can be in a certain sense very warm-hearted people, because once they become friends with strangers, they start to treat new friends like family; by the way Japanese can be very loyal friends if the circumstances permit it. For instance, It could be an amazing experience seeing someone familiar changing so drastically with their attitude, actions, and conduct toward their colleagues at a party.

The concept of true personality and false front is a typical scenario that reflects this attitude: 「本音(ほんね)」 true personality and 「建前(たてまえ), false front. This concept can also mean they say nice words and compliments to others to build better and more beneficial relationships with others, but a Westerner shouldn't forget that they often hide their true intentions.

Japanese people can be complicated and things have been changing quickly in modern Japan; many developments of their culture and society are still in the adaptation process. Furthermore, their vocabulary and even some of the standards of Japanese language are changing to catch up with modern society. Additionally, they use many everyday expressions which may sound familiar to English, but they use it in different situations. These kinds of expressions need to be studied separately.

For example:

沈黙(ちんもく)は金(きん) Silence is gold.

出(で)る杭(くい)は打(う)たれる The nail that sticks out gets hammered in.

能(のう)ある鷹(たか)は爪(つめ)を隠(かく)す Wise hawks hide their claws.

There is a well-known concept to separate inside (内(うち)) and outside (外(そと)) which tells you something about Japanese society.

Follow This Easy Reading Guide

This book focuses on enhancing reading your Japanese skills and general understanding of the language. It contains fifty short stories, and each story is subdivided into chapters per story. Each sentence in Japanese has a corresponding English translation which comes in paragraphs and blocks. You should read every sentence, and compare them to the Japanese characters above the sentence and also try to memorize the Kanji. Some stories are concentrated on dialogue. These stories include loads of natural dialogue, so you can learn conversational expressions as you read.

More about Japanese writing and communication styles

The stories are written in typical Katakana, Hiragana plus approx. 250 basic Kanji sign-characters which are for the advanced beginner and intermediate level, which is about equivalent to JLPT N4 to N5 levels.

The phonetic guide in Hiragana or the so-called Furigana can be seen in the Kanji characters, an English translation is listed beneath each paragraph or sentence. A typical Kanji character has different pronunciations and sometimes even multiple meanings. Sometimes Kanji characters are extended by Jukugo, which means Kanji characters are combined with other Kanji characters and are used to make different words and meanings. These are called Jukugo. Therefore, all the approx. 250 Kanji characters can vary a lot. The important thing for the learner is to memorize the Kanjis and compare them with the word or phrase above in the characters and text.

It is worth studying the Kanji characters, because they are considered the "soul" of the Japanese language, it is estimated there are approx.

6,000 Kanji characters in total in Japanese. A typical Japanese book lists between 2,500 and 3,500 Kanji characters for a typical novel while newspapers, articles and technical reports have usually under 2000.

Beware of Styles And Expressions

You could have seen or listened to the words desu and masu which are the traditional Japanese language styles.

This book covers the most common styles of Japanese such as polite or official style (desu and masu) and on the other side the casual/ plain (da) style, since many short stories are based on descriptions odd situations and dialogues.

Most newspaper articles or business letters are usually written in da/dearu style because it's a plain style and written language. The da style includes a plain, casual speaking style that often describes situations while the da style is more common as a form of expression, especially when it comes to fiction. But for the writing itself the dearu style (plain) is most often used. When you make conversations with people you usually speak in desu/masu style. It can be confusing, but it should be mentioned, because desu/masu is one of the three types of Japanese honorifics, also called the "polite conversation form". Nevertheless, when talking to close friends, family members or to a young(er) person the casual plain (da) style is used. However, all these details don't affect English translations. The dialogues in the stories vary in styles depending on the gender and the assumed perception with the reader.

Before You Get Started

After reviewing the sentences individually, the first step is always to memorize the characters and check if you recognize the characters in any way.

Read the sentence and compare the Japanese characters repeatedly. After repeated reading you probably start to recognize some characters. You can often guess the Japanese character simply using the context of the sentence and the rest of the story.

After reading the paragraphs or blocks of phrases, repeat reading the story and look again at the Japanese characters. Take a guess at the meaning of the character; it's not as hard as you think! If you comprehend the general meaning of the story, it's usually easier to recognize the characters.

Rather than studying all the characters at once, a handy trick is to write down new characters as good as you can and write the English meaning next to it. You kind of write a list of characters for each story. That way your reading and understanding of the characters will improve drastically. Important is that you have fun reading the stories, and always take a casual look at the characters.

Part 1: Japanese Stories for Beginners Including Hiragana, Kanji And Furigana

1. The Tokyo Fish Market

東京魚市場

Today my Japanese friend wanted to show me the highlights for tourists in Tokyo.

今日、私の日本人の友達が、東京にある観光のハイライトを見せてくれました。

Of course, I wanted to see the famous Tsukiji fish market. This market is famous for auctioning tuna.

もちろん、私は有名な築地魚市場を見たかったのです。この市場は、マグロの競りでよく知られています。

Some special tuna can reach prices that top $200,000.

貴重なマグロだと最高で$200,000の値段がつくことがあります。

We arrived in the early morning and there was already a large crowd of fish traders participating in the auction.

私たちが到着した早朝には、すでに多くの卸売業者の人々が競りに参加していました。

The fish just lay on the floor in various portions. It looked like they had placed a paper slip on all the fishes and caskets; and there was a lot of wild talk at the auction.

様々な大きさの魚が床に置かれて、その魚や箱の上には、札がありました。そして、勢いのある声がひびいていました。

I was smiling. It all looked so interesting and professional.

すべてが専門的で興味深く、私は笑顔になっていました。

I was thinking Japanese is probably not so difficult to speak; so I said a few words I thought I heard others were saying.

日本語を話すことは、そこまで難しいとは思わなかったので、私は他の人が言っていたであろう言葉を言いました。

The people started to look at me and I felt encouraged to say more Japanese words that just popped into my mind.

周りの人たちが私を見始めたので、自信が湧いてきて、さっと思いついた日本語を続けて言いました。

Suddenly, my friend gestured we should go.

すると突然、友達がもう行かなければ、とジャスチャーをしました。

We just wanted to leave when somebody said in English that I needed to pay. I didn't understand.

誰かが英語で、私が支払いをしなければならないと言ったときに、私たちはその場を離れましたが、わけが分からなくなりました。

My friend then told me, I used the Japanese word for to buy, but I said that it must have been a misunderstanding. Besides I did not have any paper slips.

すると、友だちは、私が落札するための日本語を使ったのだ、と教えてくれました。

けれども、そもそも私は札を持っていなかったのだから、それは誤解だったのだと伝えました。

The Japanese man said, It doesn't matter, my word as a foreigner was good enough to make the purchase.

すると、ある日本人(にほんじん)の男性(だんせい)が、問題(もんだい)はないよ、外国語(がいこくご)である私(わたし)の言葉(ことば)が買(か)ってもらうために十分通用(じゅうぶんつうよう)することができたからと言(い)いました。

2. Buddhism in Japan
日本の仏教

This is my first trip to this fantastic country; and today I am visiting a large Buddhist temple.
今回が、このすばらしい国への初めての旅です。そして今日、私は大きなお寺を訪れます。

I am curious, because I heard Japanese temples are different.
日本のお寺は特徴的だと聞いていたので、とてもわくわくしています。

In a beautiful public garden, I saw a large temple.
美しい公共の庭に、大きなお寺を見ました。

When I stretched my neck to see the beautiful rooftop, I felt like somebody was watching me.
美しい屋上を見ようと首を伸ばしたとき、誰かに見られているような気がしました。

To my surprise, there was a man standing next to me.
驚くことに、その人は私のすぐ隣にいる男性だったのです。

He smiled kindly, and I returned it.
彼は優しい笑顔を向け、私も笑顔を返しました。

He said that I must be someone interested in spiritual matters.
そして、私が神秘的なものに興味があるに違いない、と彼は言いました。

I replied, that I am, but was just a passing tourist. Our talk continued; and actually had an interesting conversation.

たしかにそうですが、私はたんなる観光客なのだと答えました。私たちのおもしろい会話は続きました。

He told me he was a Japanese Buddhist. What a coincidence.

偶然にも彼は日本の僧侶でした。

He also explained that there are many different schools of Buddhism.

様々なタイプの仏教の学校があると説明してくれました。

For instance, that Japanese Buddhism is more into action and that all the teaching from the old schools are already included;

例えば、日本の仏教はより行動指針を大切にしていて、古流からの教えがすべて受け継がれている。

and most importantly that I can find Buddhahood in this life! I kept asking questions.

なにより最も重要なのが、その生活の中で悟りを見つけられるということです。私は質問をし続けました。

Eventually, he said that in order to get all the benefits that Japanese Buddhism offers, one has to become part of the organization and eventually I would receive a kind of scroll; that made me think.

やがて彼は、日本の仏教が与えるすべての恩恵を受け取るためには、組織への加入が必要で、その後、私に教えを説く古書を受け取ることができる、と言いました。

Anyway, I remember, that as unexpected as the man appeared, he suddenly disappeared just like a ghost. It was a very beneficial conversation, that I know.

その後、ともかくよく覚えているのは、彼が突然現れたと思うと、すぐさま幽霊のように消え去ったことです。この会話はとても貴重なものでした。

3. Lost in Tokyo

東京で迷う

Our hotel is on the other side of Tokyo, somewhere on the outskirts of the city. My partner and I need to catch the subway for a business meeting.

私たちのホテルは、東京の反対側の郊外にありました。パートナーと私は、仕事の会議に行くために地下鉄を使わなければなりませんでした。

We are both foreigners and not familiar with the different lines. First, we got into the wrong train; and then we got off at the wrong station, after catching another train that left us stranded somewhere in the city, we were completely lost.

私たちはともに外国人で、地下鉄の路線になじみがなかったので、違う電車に乗ってしまい、違う駅に降りてしまいました。その後、市内に行く別の電車に乗ったのですが、完全に方向を失ってしまいました。

Eventually, we decided to take a taxi that drove us to the exact location.

なので、会議が行われる場所に連れて行ってもらうため、タクシーをつかまえました。

Of course we were late, but our Japanese business partners didn't mention it, and fortunately our meeting turned out to be very successful.

もちろん私たちは遅刻をしてしまったのですが、日本のビジネスパートナーの方々はそれについて何も言及せず、幸いにも会議はとても成功しました。

Nevertheless, we took the subway again to find our hotel. No chance! We were lost again until late at night,

けれども、その後は全く不運続きで、ホテルへ戻るために利用した地下鉄で再び、夜中まで迷ってしまったのです。

but we saw many wonderful and amazing train stations. Many of them had elegant shops and little shopping malls connected to the stations. So we spent a lot of time shopping and almost forgot that we were lost.

ただ、きれいなお店や小さなショッピングモールが連結された、すてきな駅を発見し、そこでショッピングをすることができたので、ほとんど迷子になっていることを忘れていました。

Somewhere, we got out, and decided to sleep in another hotel near an unknown train station. However, I must say, we had a very good time in Tokyo.

最終的にはどこか外に出て、名前も知らない駅の近くにあった別のホテルに宿泊することになってしまいました。けれども、私は間違いなく、東京でとてもよい時間を過ごすことができました。

4. Teaching in Japan

日本(にほん)で教師(きょうし)をする

My name is Jessica. I am from Toronto, and I can say with confidence that I already speak Japanese very well.

私(わたし)の名前(なまえ)はジェシカ、トロント出身(しゅっしん)です。日本語(にほんご)を上手(じょうず)に話(はな)すことができると自信(じしん)を持(も)っています。

For some time, I have been trying to find a teaching job in Japan, but I didn't want just any teaching job.

以前(いぜん)より、日本(にほん)で教師(きょうし)の仕事(しごと)を探(さが)していますが、教師(きょうし)の仕事(しごと)であればなんでもいいわけではありません。

I was trying to find an English teaching position in a school with an excellent reputation which could help me to further my career.

私(わたし)が探(さが)しているのは、将来(しょうらい)のキャリアにつながる、評価(ひょうか)の高(たか)い学校(がっこう)での英語(えいご)の教師(きょうし)としての役職(やくしょく)です。

I received a personal tip from a Japanese friend that eventually helped me to land a good job in a very good school.

のちに、すばらしい学校(がっこう)での仕事(しごと)を見(み)つけてくれた日本人(にほんじん)の友(とも)だちから、個人的(こじんてき)なこつを教(おそ)わりました。

I was teaching in a mid level high school, and my students were very motivated.

私(わたし)は、高校(こうこう)の中学年(ちゅうがくねん)を教(おし)えていて、生徒(せいと)たちはとても熱心(ねっしん)でした。

Sometimes I had to watch my back, because a school is a business, and I didn't want to get fired because some jealous administrator tried to spread lies about me as is common in many schools.

ただ、学校もビジネスの場である ので、解雇されないように気をつけなければなりません。

というのも、他の学校でも共通するように、嫉妬心を持った事務の人が、私について嘘のうわさを広げようとしていたのです。

After all, I recommend that any foreigner teach in Japan, just for the experience.

つまるところ、外国の人々にとって日本での教師の仕事は、経験としてのみお勧めをします。

5. Karaoke Japanese Style
日本のカラオケスタイル

My friend and I are trying to find an inexpensive karaoke bar just for a couple of hours to have fun. The good and affordable ones you can find best when asking students or friends.

私と友達は、数時間楽しむためにあまり高くないカラオケバーを探しています。一番お手頃価格でいいと、学生や友達たちがおすすめしてくれるものです。

Advertising can be deceptive, especially in Japan. Eventually we found a suspicious establishment in a high rise building on the six floor, the entrance and corridors looked pretty much like an apartment floor.

特に日本では広告は当てになりません。ついに私たちは、6階建の何やら怪しい雰囲気のビルにあるカラオケを発見しました。入り口や通路はいったて普通のアパートメントのようでした。

After paying the fee, we arrived at our box, which was a little room on the 5th floor; it had a little table, a couch, a microphone, and a TV.

料金を支払った後、5階に位置する、小さなテーブル、ソファー、マイクそしてテレビがある部屋に入りました。

As expected the equipment was easy to handle. So we sang our songs, danced and had fun.

装備されているものは思っていたより使いやすかったです。
なので、歌って、踊って、楽しむことができました。

As we left our box, we encountered a drunken foreigner. He asked us if we can give him a massage. We laughed and rejected his request.

部屋を離れた後、酔っている外国人に出会いました。彼は、何かメッセージをくれないかと言いましたが、わたしたちは笑って彼のリクエストを断りました。

6. Saving Face

面目を保つ

I arrived about a month ago, and finally have been hired to do an advertising gig. No career breakthrough, but a start.

私は1ヶ月前に到着し、ついに広告会社での仕事が決まりました。キャリアのバックラウンドはありませんが、とりあえず始めてみたのです。

Sometimes, foreigners in Japan are hired for all kinds of reasons.

日本にいる外国の人々はさまざまな理由で雇用されます。

Before I went to the meet-up, I remembered the custom that you need to dress well accordingly and to your status.

面接に行く前、状況に合わせて身なりを整えるという習慣があることを思い出しました。

I wore lots of jewelry to make an impression.

なので、私は強い印象を残すことができるよう、たくさんのジュエリーを身につけました。

Even on the street, some people gave me funny looks. Were these people looking down at me?

道では、人々が私を見て変な表情をしていました。私を見下しているのでしょうか?

Sometimes I was thinking who the hell are you, staring at me?

たまに、私を凝視している人たちはなんて失礼なんだ、とさえ思いました。

I think of myself as someone who can adapt to a different culture. In Rome, do as the Romans do, I thought.

郷に入っては郷に従え、というように、私は異なる文化に合わすことができる人物だ

と思っていました。

When people asked me something, I preferred to answer, "How interesting!"

何か人が質問をするとき、私は「おもしろいですね!」を答える方が好きです。

Anyway, the advertising gig went well, and I got paid punctually.

ともかく、広告会社での仕事はうまく行き、きちんと給料も支払われました。

A person from that company gave me advice. "Building your reputation comes first" and "Never point other people's mistakes out". Isn't it funny?

会社のある人が私に「あなた自身の評価を積み上げることがまず大事」「人々の誤りを指摘してはいけません」と、アドバイスをくれました。これは、おかし

いとは思いませんか?

7. Faux Pas in the restaurant
レストランでの失態

Even before I traveled to Japan, I heard that I'd have to change shoes if I go to the toilet. You can bring your own slippers or sandals, but most often, you can get a pair of slippers that are lying around at the toilet entrance.

日本へ旅行する前から、トイレに行く際にはスリッパに履き替えなければならない、ということを知っていました。自分のスリッパやサンダルを持ち運ぶこともできますが、大抵はトイレの入り口にスリッパが置かれています。

But one night in Osaka, when I went to a nice traditional Japanese restaurant, I had to go to the toilet, but couldn't find any slippers near the toilet entrance.

しかしながら、ある夜、大阪にある伝統的な和食のレストランでのことですが、私がトイレに行ったとき、入り口にスリッパがないことに気がついたのです。

I opened the toilet door and winked to my wife in the restaurant, asking her what to do. She said, "Don't worry, just take your shoes off."

妻にウインクをしながらどのようにするかわかる？と聞き、トイレのドアを開けました。妻は「心配しないで、まずは靴を脱ぐのでしょう。」と答えました。

That's what I did, and after using the toilet I walked back into the restaurant area.

実際に 私 もその通りにして、トイレが終わった後、レストランのエリアに戻って行きました。

When I arrived at the table my wife laughed out loud, but all the Japanese customers gave me a funny look.

テーブルについたとき、妻は大いに笑い、日本人の客たちは 私 をこっけいに見ていました。

Suddenly a waiter came from behind with a mop.

そしてすぐさまウェイターが 私 の後ろからモップを持って近づいてきました。

I turned around, and I saw my own wet footprints on the polished floor.

振り返ると、磨かれた床の上に 私 の濡れた足跡があったのです。

On the way back from the toilet I had forgotten to put my socks and shoes on; and frankly, the man's toilet floor was very wet, which was of no surprise, considering that I had a bladder problem.

そしてようやく、帰り際にソックスとシューズを履き忘れていたことに気がつきました。実のところ、男性トイレの床はとても濡れていてたのですが、私の膀胱に問題があると思われても驚きではないかもしれません。

8. Just a couple of drinks

何杯かのお酒

I remember when I was a student I had to share my dormitory room on campus with a Japanese student.

私が学生のころ、学校の寮で日本人の学生と部屋を共有していました。

We didn't talk much first; the truth is we were both very busy. I tried to ask her questions.

始めのころはお互い忙しかったので、あまり話をしませんでした。

私はいくつか彼女に質問をしました。

Some of them were personal and perhaps a little too much for her comfort. She always seemed to hesitate with her answers, until she gave a very deliberate answer.

中には彼女にとっては個人的すぎる情報もあったかもしれません。慎重に答えを出すまで、いつもためらっているようでした。

I wanted to overcome this invisible barrier; so on a Friday night I asked her if she wanted to go out and join me for a drink.

私はこの見えない壁を打ち破りたかったので、金曜日の夜、飲みに行こうとさそいました。

After a few drinks, she became very friendly and opened up. She talked about herself.

何杯か飲んだあと、彼女は自身について語ってくれるほど、とても親しく心を開いてくれるようになりました。

However, she became drunk after just a few more glasses. She almost fell asleep at the bar.

しかしながら、もう数杯か飲んだ後、彼女は酔っ払ってしまい、バーで寝てしまいました。

Strangers had to help carry her into the taxi.

近くにいた人が、彼女をタクシーまで運んでくれるのを手伝ってくれました。

Later, I found out that Japanese people are unable to drink as much as Western people. Their livers work slower.

後で私は、日本人の肝臓の働きはゆっくりしていて、欧米の人と比べるとあまりお酒を飲むことができない、ということを知りました。

I don't know if that's true, or maybe Japanese people are just special people.

真実かどうかは分かりませんが、おそらく日本人は特別なのだと思います。

9. Humor is if you still laugh

ユーモアは笑(わら)っているときに

I wanted to go to Japan for a long time. I never met a real Japanese person in my country.

私(わたし)は長(なが)い間(あいだ)、日本(にほん)に行(い)きたいと思(おも)っていました。私(わたし)がいる国(くに)では、今(いま)まで日本人(にほんじん)に会(あ)ったことがありません。

When I finally arrived for the first time in Japan, I noticed all these serious faces.

とうとう、初(はじ)めて日本(にほん)に到着(とうちゃく)したとき、私(わたし)はたくさんの人々(ひとびと)が真剣(しんけん)な顔(かお)をしていることに気(き)がつきました。

Even in the trains, there was not much speaking.

電車(でんしゃ)の中(なか)であっても、誰(だれ)も話(はなし)をしていません。

Sometimes, I nodded at strangers. I wanted to talk to them, make some friends on the trip like I did in so many other countries.

ときどき、日本人(にほんじん)にお辞儀(じぎ)をしました。他(ほか)の国(くに)での旅行(りょこう)で友達(ともだち)をつくったときのように、私(わたし)は話(はな)しかけたかったのです。

In Italy and in Brazil, starting a conversation with strangers was never an issue.

イタリアやブラジルでは、初(はじ)めて会(あ)う人々(ひとびと)と会話(かいわ)をするのに、何(なに)も問題(もんだい)はありませんでした。

I decided I needed to break the ice, to get some life into their heads, so to speak. How about some humor from a real human being, not from a TV comedy? So, one morning, I stepped into the subway train.

なので、私はこの氷をとかし、会話をする決心をしました。テレビのコメディ番組ではなく、目の前にいる人間によるユーモアはおもしろいかもしれない？と考え、ある朝、地下鉄に乗りました。

I saw all these serious faces, nobody seemed to be alive.
いたるところにある真剣な顔、誰も生きている気配がありません。

I took a deep breath, and shouted: "Hi, I am Japanese, I am Japanese!"
大きく息をすいこみ、「こんにちは、私は日本人です、日本人です！」とさけびました。

But nobody was laughing. I shouted a little louder so they would understand the humor.
しかし、だれも笑わなかったので、ユーモアをわかってもらえるよう、私は少し声を大きくしてさけびました。

A man said something I couldn't understand, but it wasn't a friendly remark, that I could tell.
ある男性が、はっきりとはわからなかったのですが、あまり親しくない様子で何かを言いました。

Suddenly, a woman accused me in English of being a liar. I told her this was a joke. She didn't believe me, and repeated I was a liar.
すると突然、女性が英語で私が嘘をついていると言いました。私が彼女にこれは冗談であると説明しましたが、彼女は信じず、嘘つきだと言い続けました。

The next morning, I flew to Brazil.

そして翌朝、私はブラジルに帰りました。

10. A special Geisha

特別な芸者

We had been planning this restaurant meeting for weeks.
Just a day before the meeting, someone called me and asked me if I needed a Geisha to keep the conversation with all the guests going.

私たちはこの食事会を数週間かけて計画していました。数週間前、誰かが私に電話で、ゲストとの会話を保つために芸者が必要であるか聞いてきました。

The restaurant meeting went as expected. Eventually the Geisha showed up and surprised the group with a typical dress, a white powdered face, and a soft speaking voice.

レストランでの食事会はうまくいっていました。しばらくすると、芸者が着物を着て、白粉を塗った独特な姿で、柔らかい声で話しながら入ってきたので、みんなは驚きました。

Later, after dinner was taken, she entertained the guests with her wit and made sure the conversations didn't get boring.

食事が終わった後、芸者はゲストに気を使い、会話がつまらなくならないようにしてくれました。

Later that night, she even showed us a typical Geisha dance and music.

夜遅くには、典型的な芸者の歌と踊りを見せてくれました。

However, after the last guest went home, she continued the conversation with me in English, which was good enough to keep me listening.

けれども、最後のゲストが帰った後、彼女は私に英語で話し続けました。私はただ聞いたのですが、

From what I gathered, she wanted to ask me if she should change her dress for a different dress, and if she could go with me to my place.
彼女はさらに、別の服に着替えて私の宿泊先に行きましょうか、とさえ言ってきたのです。

However, I just thanked her for her time and left.
私は丁寧にお礼を言って断り、帰路につきました。

11. A happy marriage
幸(しあわ)せな結婚(けっこん)

My name is Berta. I've been married to Bill for almost eight years. My husband is a successful businessman and often travels to Japan.

私(わたし)の名前(なまえ)はベルタです。ビルと結婚(けっこん)して8年(ねん)になります。夫(おっと)は成功(せいこう)しているビジネスマンで、よく日本(にほん)への出張(しゅっちょう)があるため、

I am a housewife. My husband travels between Japan and California regularly.

日本(にっぽん)とカリフォルニアの間(あいだ)をひんぱんに旅(たび)をしています。私(わたし)は専業主婦(せんぎょうしゅふ)です。

We don't have children. When he is at home, we do a lot of things together.

私(わたし)たちには子(こ)どもがいません。夫(おっと)が家(いえ)にいるときには、

私(わたし)たちは一緒(いっしょ)にたくさんのことをします。夕食(ゆうしょく)を外(そと)ですることがとても好(す)きです。

We love to go out for dinner. My husband is a very romantic and caring person. We do also have our differences.

夫(おっと)は とてもロマンティックで愛情深(あいじょうぶか)い人(ひと)です。お互(たが)い異(こと)なることもあります。

My husband is very sporty and he goes to the gym regularly. I, on the other hand, like to get up late and enjoy watching TV.

夫(おっと)はスポーツが好(す)きでよくジムに行(い)きますが、私(わたし)は朝遅(あさおそ)くに起(お)きてテレビを見(み)ること

が好(す)きです。

Unfortunately, I am overweight, but I have promised my husband to start a diet. Recently, he came home early and caught me in the basement where I was indulging in candies.

残念なことにその結果、太ってしまいました。しかし、私はダイエットをすると夫に約束をしました。最近では、彼が家に早く帰ってきて、こっそりと地下室でキャンディを食べているところを見つかってしまいました。

12. Under the lamp post

街灯の下で

Hiroto is Japanese and lives in Amsterdam. Hiroto works quite hard for an international shipping company. Sometimes he even has to work late into the night.

ヒロトはアムステルダムに住んでいる日本人です。彼はインターナショナルな海運会社で熱心に働いています。たまに、彼は夜遅くまで働かなければならないことがあります。

He lives alone. Every night when Hiroto goes home, he takes a shortcut through a park to reach his apartment.

彼は一人暮らしです。毎晩家に帰るとき、公園を横切って近道をします。

It is late autumn now and winter is approaching soon. When he goes home through the park in the evening, the lamps are already lit.

今は、晩秋でもうすぐ冬が近づいてきます。夕方の帰路では、すでに公園のライトが灯っています。

One evening Hiroto as he walks through the park again, he notices a young woman standing under a lamp post. The woman seems to be waiting for someone. Hiroto finds the woman very attractive.

ある晩、ヒロトが公園を通っているとき、若い女性が街灯の下で立っているのを見ました。彼女はだれかを待っているようでした。とても魅力的でした。

The next evening that same woman is standing again under the same lamp post. When Hiroto goes to bed, he still thinks of the pretty woman.

次の日の晩にも、同じ女性は同じ街灯の下で立っていました。彼は寝床についたとき、

すてきなその女性のことを思いました。

He's noticed she always wears high heels.

そして、彼女がいつもハイヒールを履いていることに気がつきました。

Over the next few weeks he sees the woman in the park, but Hiroto is too shy to speak to the woman. Besides, it is not custom for a Japanese man doesn't talk to strangers.

数週間後、彼は再びその女性を公園で見ましたが、恥じらいから話しかけること

ができませんでした。それに、日本の男性にとって、見知らぬ人に声をかけることは、

習慣ではないのです。

On a Friday night, Hiroto approaches the woman. Today he wants to talk to her. The woman smiles at Hiroto. Then she asks him, "Are you going to come with me?"

金曜日の夜、ヒロトはついに彼女に近寄ります。今日はいよいよ

彼女に話しかけるのです。女性は彼に微笑み、そして「私とどこかに行きますか？」と

彼をさそいました。

13. Group learning
グループ学習

My name is Lisa. I have lived in Tokyo for almost three years.
私の名前はリサです。東京に3年間ほど住んでいます。

I came to Japan with my best friend, because we wanted to work as English language teachers in Japan.
一緒に英語の教師として働きたかったので、私の親友と日本にきました。

When I arrived, I couldn't speak a word of Japanese.
着いたときは、私は日本語を一言も話すことができませんでした。

Therefore, before we could become English teachers, we first had to learn some basic Japanese.
なので、英語の教師になる前にまず、基礎の日本語を学ぶ必要がありました。

We take lessons every evening in a Japanese language school. Sometimes I don't understand everything but then I'll ask the teacher. "Can you please speak a little more slowly?"
私たちは毎晩日本語学校でレッスンを受けました。たまに、分からないことがある際には、先生に「もう少しゆっくりと話していただけますか?」とお願いしました。

If the teacher speaks slowly I understand almost everything.
Fortunately, my Japanese has improved a lot since I've begun learning in a group, which is a more fun way to learn.
先生がゆっくりと話すと、私はほとんどすべて理解できました。幸い、グループレッスンといった、とても面白い学習方法で日本語を学び始めてから、私の日本語は

とても上達しました。

I look forward to my next classes and even more important; I am really happy to be teaching the English language to others in the near future.
私は次のクラスも楽しみにしています。そして一番大切なのは、
近い将来、英語を教えられることをとてもうれしく思っていることです。

14. I marry my office

私は仕事と結婚する

Mr. Meyer is an accountant and works for a large company. He has regular working hours. Mr. Meyer starts his day at eight o'clock and at five o'clock he leaves his office.

メイヤー氏は会計士として大企業で働いています。彼には、8時始業、17時終業と決まった労働時間があります。

Lately, Mr. Meyer seems ill. His colleagues say that he does not seem focused.

最近の彼は体調が良くないように思われ、同僚たちは、仕事に集中できていないと言っています。

What nobody knows is that Mr. Meyer has a secret. A short while ago Mr. Meyer met his new girlfriend and real secret is that he met her on the street.

誰も知らないことは、彼が秘密を持っていることです。少し前、彼は新しい彼女に出会いました。実のところ、彼女と出会ったのは道なのです。

Actually, Mr. Meyer has paid money for her time.

彼は、彼女との時間にお金を費やしています。

One day, Mr. Meyer tells his colleague that he's going to get married soon.

ある日、メイヤー氏が同僚に、そろそろ結婚をすると言いました。

But this colleague who has observed Mr. Meyer and thinks he knows something, tells the boss that Mr. Meyer plans to marry a woman of questionable reputation.

けれども、メイヤー氏を監察していたこの同僚は何か怪しいと考え、上司に、彼が問題があるかもしれない女性と結婚しようとしていると報告しました。

The boss tells Mr. Meyer that he is no longer allowed to work for the company when he marries this woman.

すると、この上司はメイヤー氏に、その女性と結婚するのであれば、ここで働くことをいっさい許さない、と告げました。

Mr. Meyer thinks carefully about his options. Should he marry the woman or keep the job?

メイヤー氏は慎重に考えました。この女性と結婚すべきなのか？それとも、仕事を守るべきなのか？

Finally, he tells his boss, "I am going to get married, but not to this woman, instead I will marry my office."

そして、彼は上司に、「私は結婚をします。けれども、彼女とではなく、私のオフィスとです。」と伝えました。

15. A Spanish Restaurant in Tokyo

ダイアログー今日(きょう)うさぎがある

Fernando has a Spanish restaurant in Tokyo. His restaurant is part of a large house where he also lives. Behind the house is a large, wild garden.

フェルナンドは東京(とうきょう)でスペインレストランを持(も)っています。彼(かれ)のレストランは、大(おお)きな自宅(じたく)の一部(いちぶ)にあり、家(いえ)の後(うし)ろには大(おお)きな自然(しぜん)な庭(にわ)があります。

One night, when Fernando just wants to close his restaurant, guests came in late.

ある夜(よる)、フェルナンドがレストランを閉(し)めようとしたとき、お客(きゃく)さんが入(はい)ってきました。

His Japanese wife works in the kitchen. She wonders why her husband wants to serve customers so late.

彼(かれ)の日本人(にほんじん)の奥(おく)さんはキッチンで働(はたら)いていて、なぜ夫(おっと)がこんな遅(おそ)くにお客(きゃく)さんにサービスをしたがっているのか疑問(ぎもん)に思(おも)っていました。

"Why do you still want to serve guests," she asks. "It's late and I'll never get out of the kitchen again."

「どうして、まだお客(きゃく)さんにサービスをしたいの?もう遅(おそ)いし、私(わたし)はキッチンから出(で)られなくなってしまうじゃない。」と彼女(かのじょ)が言(い)いました。

"The guests have already ordered wine," says Fernando. "Plus, we still have a rabbit in the fridge. So I told the guests tonight that I only have rabbit."

するとフェルナンドは「お客(きゃく)さんはもうワインを注文(ちゅうもん)してしまった。それに、まだ冷蔵(れいぞう)

庫に一羽うさぎが残っている。だからお客さんには、今夜はうさぎだけある、と伝えたんだ。」と答えました。

16. Dining European Style
ダイアログーヨーロッパスタイルのダイニング

Unlike in the US, in many European countries a customer can just enter a restaurant and choose an available seat where you feel comfortable.

アメリカとは違（ちが）って、ヨーロッパ国々（くにぐに）には、お客（きゃく）がレストランに入（はい）ると、空（あ）いてる快適（てき）そうな席（せき）を自分（じぶん）で選（えら）ぶ習慣（しゅうかん）があります。

However, in more upscale restaurants most often there are no menus on the table, so you would have to ask the waiter to bring you one.

高級（こうきゅう）なレストランでは、テーブルの上（うえ）にはメニューがないことがほとんどなので、ウェイターに持（も）ってきてもらうようたのみます。

The waiters usually wear a white shirt and black trousers. They also carry a little notebook to notate orders.
Often a conversation between a customer and a waiter follows this pattern:

ウェイターはだいたい、白（しろ）のシャツを着（き）て黒（くろ）のズボンを履（は）いて、オーダーを取（と）るための小（ちい）さなメモ帳（ちょう）を持（も）っています。お客（きゃく）とウェイターの会話（かいわ）はたいていこのようなパターンです。

Waiter: "Good evening, have you already found something that you would like to order?"

ウェイター：こんばんは。ご注文（ちゅうもん）はお決（き）まりでしょうか？

Customer: "I will take a schnitzel and a salad, number 5 on the menu."

お客（きゃく）：メニュー番号（ばんごう）5の、シュニッツェルとサラダにします。

Waiter: "That's okay. What would you like to drink?"

ウェイター：かしこまりました。お飲みものはいかがなさいますか？

Customer: "Just mineral water."

お客：ミネラルウォーターでお願いします。

Waiter: "With or without gas?"

ウェイター：ガス入りでしょうか、ガスなしでしょうか？

Customer. "Still water, with little gas."

お客：少しだけガスの入ったミネラルウォーターをお願いします。

Waiter: "So you want a salad, a schnitzel and a mineral water with little gas, correct?"

ウェイター：はい、それではサラダ、シュニッツェルと少しガスの入ったミネラルウォーターですね？

The customer nods. After the meal, the customer asks: " Bill please."

お客はうなずきます。食事のあと、お客は「お会計をお願いします。」と言います。

A tip is always voluntary and in most countries is not included in the bill.

チップはたいてい任意で、多くの国では支払いにふくまれていません。

17. The Tourist guide
観光ガイド

My name is Yuto and I live in Okinawa. On the weekends I show American tourists and US military personell the city.

私の名前はゆうとで、沖縄に住んでいます。週末には、アメリカの観光客とアメリカ軍にいる人たちに街を案内します。

I speak English well because I used to work at a Toyota plant in the USA.

アメリカにあるTOYOTAの工場で働いていたので、私は英語を上手に話すことができます。

I'm retired now actually. To supplement my pension, I work from Friday to Sunday as a tourist guide.

年金の補足のため、金曜日と土曜日に観光ガイドとして働いているので、実のところ今疲れています。

Last weekend, I had a large group of foreign retirees to whom I showed the city. I walked them around and explained the history of the city.

先週、大きな定年退職者のグループを街へ案内し、街の歴史を説明しました。

Many foreigners are interested in good restaurants and botanical gardens. Sometimes at the end of the tour, the people ask me personal questions;

多くの観光客は、おいしいレストランと植物園に興味を持っていました。ツアーの最後にはよく、個人的な質問をされます。

for example where I come from and why do I speak English so well.

例えば、私がどこから来て、どうして英語を上手に話すことができるのか、など。

I give them the perfect answer because you always have to have the right answer. That's something I have learned in America.

常に正確な答えを持っておかなければならないので、私はいつもその人たちに、完璧に答えます。これは、私がアメリカで学んだことのひとつです。

18. Inexpensive shopping in Japan

高くない日本での買い物

My name is Rachel and today I'm going to shop at the Japanese supermarket. As a student in Japan, I do not have much money and therefore must save on food.

私の名前はレイチェルです。今日、私は日本のスーパーマーケットへ買い物に行くつもりです。学生として日本にいるので、あまりお金がなく、食費を節約しています。

In addition, I support my mother in my home country. I mainly eat fish and vegetables. It's my so-called sushi diet.

それに、私は母国にいる母を支えています。主に私は魚と野菜を食べます。これは私にとって、寿司ダイエット、と言えます。

Luckily, these items are relatively inexpensive to buy in Japan. In the morning hours the supermarkets are usually not as crowded.

幸い、これらの食材は日本では比較的高くないのです。

朝の時間帯のスーパーマーケットは混んでいません。

Today I need to buy rice, vegetables, tuna and pasta. If I find something less expensive, I buy more. Changed wording and punctuation I buy only a little, which I feel means something more for the Japanese.

今日私は、お米、野菜、マグロそしてパスタを買わなければいけません。もし何かより高くないものがあれば追加して買います。私は少しだけ買い物をしますが、日本人からすると多いかもしれません。

19. Born in Michigan

ミシガン生まれ

I was born in Flint, Michigan, but to tell the truth I never felt very comfortable in this old city. Fortunately, I traveled a lot when I was still a teenager.

私はミシガンのフリントに生まれました。けれども、本音をいうと、私はこの古い街を快適だと思ったことがありません。幸い、10代のときに旅行をたくさんしました。

My parents used to live in Japan and we had a chance to see many different areas in Asia.

両親はかつて日本に住んでいたので、アジアの様々な国を訪れる機会もありました。

Since I can remember, Japan and its culture has always fascinated me. Japan has an old history and many traditions, and I remember it wasn't always easy to adapt to this culture, especially my mother had problems learning the language.

日本とその文化にはいつも感動します。けれども古い歴史とたくさんの伝統がありその文化に合わせることは簡単ではありませんでした。特に母は、言語を学ぶことに問題がありました。

Anyway, having lived there has affected my personality.

いずれにせよ、そこで暮らした経験は、私の性格に影響を与えました。

When I got a little older I started to travel by myself, for instance I traveled all the way down to Central America by car.

少し大きくなってから、私は一人で旅をするようになりました。例えば、車で中央アメリカまで南下したことがあります。

These trips were of course more adventurous than ordinary travels.

こういった旅行はもちろん、普通の旅行に比べるとより冒険的です。

I can honestly say that having visited foreign countries and traveling in general is educating in many ways.

外国を訪れ旅行することで、いろいろなことを学ぶことができます。

If you need to adapt to a foreign culture you are actually improving your social skills! I also think that international experiences make you more flexible and are good for the brain.

外国の文化に合わせる必要がある場面ではあなたの社会的なスキルが向上しているのです。また、海外での経験は、より柔軟性が身につき、思考にも良い影響を与えます。

20. Easter
イースター

Easter in England and Europe, in general, is a holiday that involves the whole family.

イギリスやヨーロッパでのイースターとは、基本的には、家族と過ごす休暇です。

On Good Friday in the countryside they often make bonfires where family and friends gather for some barbecue and sometimes music is played.

金曜日田舎の方では家族や友達が集まり、かがり火を囲いながらバーベキューをしたり音楽をしたりします。

The Easter Festival is a tradition in many countries.

多くの国では、イースターは伝統的なお祭りです。

For children, Easter morning is actually the most important day of the festival.
In the morning hours children love to paint hard boiled eggs and hide them in the bushes. They make a game out of it to find the hidden eggs,

子どもにとっては、イースターの朝は、祭りの中でもとっても重要な日です。子どもたちはゆで卵に色をつけ茂みの中に隠し、その隠された卵を探すという遊びをします。

but not all of the eggs are always found. Even weeks after Easter, there are times when the land stinks of rotten eggs that haven't been found.

しかし、すべての卵が探し出されるわけではありません。イースターが終わった数週間後であっても、庭から発見されなかった腐った卵の匂いがすることがあります。

21. Foreigners in Britain

イギリスにいる外国人

In England there are many landmarks for sightseeing trips and popular tourist destinations in general.

イギリスではたくさんの観光のランドマークがあり、観光客にとって人気の場所です。

Probably the most visited cities by foreign tourists are London, Brighton, Yorkshire and probably Britain's most visited sightseeing spot is the mysterious Stonehenge.

おそらく、最も観光客が多い都市は、ロンドン、ブライトン、そしてヨークシャーでしょう。また、訪問者数が一番多いスポットはミステリアスなストーンヘンジです。

Most foreign visitors want to stay in London as there are hundreds of famous places to see.

ほとんどの観光客は、数多くの有名なスポットがあるロンドンに滞在したいと考えます。

Westminster Abbey, Big Ben, the Buckingham Palace, Piccadilly Circus, and the British Museum are probably even some of the most visited places worldwide.

ウェストミンスター寺院、ビッグベン、バッキンガム宮殿、ピカデリー・サーカス、そして英国博物館は世界で最も訪れられている場所です。

London alone has over nineteen million visitors per year and since the British Pound has fallen sharply over the last few years, the UK will continue to be a very popular destination.

ロンドンには、1年間で1900万人もの観光客が訪れます。
さらに、ここ数年間イギリスのパウンドが下落しているので、
イギリスはこれからも外国人にとって人気の観光地となるでしょう。

The most common reason why foreigners like Britain is probably its culture, for instance tea time, pub culture, and the Queen but also its history that seems to be everywhere and connected to everything in their culture.

外国人がイギリスを好きな理由として共通しているのは、おそらくその文化です。例えば、ティータイム、パブ、そして女王。そして、その文化につながる歴史も多くの人々をひきつける理由です。

22. Kindness

優(やさ)しさ

Steven is a movie buff. Today is Friday and for this evening he plans to go to a theater to watch a newly released movie.

スティーブは熱狂的(ねっきょうてき)な映画(えいが)のファンです。金曜日(きんようび)の今日(きょう)、彼(かれ)は新(あたら)しくリリースされる映画(えいが)を見(み)るために、夕方映画館(ゆうがたえいがかん)に行(い)く予定(よてい)です。

Steven arrives at the theater early, but there is already a long line in front of the box office.

少(すこ)し早(はや)く映画館(えいがかん)に着(つ)いたのですが、すでに長(なが)い行列(ぎょうれつ)がチケット売(う)り場(ば)の前(まえ)にありました。

Interestingly, there are also many elderly people waiting in line. That's probably because on weekends they also show a few classic movies.

おもしろいことに、その列(れつ)にはたくさんのお年寄(としよ)りが並(なら)んで待(ま)っていました。おそらく週末(しゅうまつ)には昔(むかし)の映画(えいが)を少(すこ)し上映(じょうえい)しているからでしょう。

Although the movie Steve wants to see starts in a few minutes, he offers an elderly couple to go before him. He understands well that it must be hard for them to stay in line, especially because of the rainy weather.

スティーブが見(み)たい映画(えいが)は数分後(すうふんご)に始(はじ)まるのですが、彼(かれ)は雨(あめ)の中(なか)長(なが)い間(あいだ)待(ま)つのは大変(たいへん)だろうと思(おも)って、お年寄(としよ)りの夫婦(ふうふ)に先(さき)をゆずりました。

Steve is still staying in line as he sees a piece of paper on the floor. He takes a closer looks and discovers that the paper is actually a twenty dollar bill.

床にある紙を見つけたとき、彼はまだ列に並んでいました。彼が近寄ってよく見ると、それが20ドル札であることに気がつきました。

He picks up the money and wonders if somebody in front of him might have dropped it.

それを手に取り、もしかすると前にいた人の誰かが落としたのかもしれない、と思いました。

The elderly couple watches him. Suddenly they approach him. "It might well be that we just dropped the money by accident. But since you are such a kind person, it's all yours."

するとお年寄りの夫婦が彼を見て突然近寄ってきたのです。

そして「おそらくそれは私たちが落としたお金なのですが、あなたはとても親切な方なので、そのお金はあなたのものです。」と言いました。

23. My Hobbies

私の趣味

My name is Minako and I have many hobbies. The reason is simple; I just have many different interests.

私の名前はみなこです。私にはたくさんの趣味があります。理由は簡単で、ただ単にいろいろなことに興味があるからです。

As a kid I had a large doll and toys collection, but now my likes have changed. Nowadays I am very much interested in Japanese art.

幼いころ、私は大きな人形とおもちゃのコレクションを持っていました。

今では趣味は変わって、日本のアートに興味を持っています。

I also like to paint with water-colors and I am especially fond of reading manga books. Actually, I like to read all kinds of nonfiction books, even cooking books. I also like to play the guitar. Music is one of my favorite pastimes.

水彩画をすることや漫画を読むことが好きです。ノンフィクションの本や、料理の本を読むこと、ギターを弾くことも好きです。音楽は私のお気に入りの娯楽です。

Being involved with many activities is actually a tradition in our family. My sister Rai likes to read books about philosophy and everyone in my family likes to travel..

多くのアクティビティをすることは、実は私の家族の伝統なのです。私の姉のレイは哲学の本を読むことが好きで、家族のみんなは旅行が大好きです

Besides reading and music, I also like to go swimming in one of the many public swimming pools

さらに、本(ほん)を読(よ)むことや音楽(おんがく)、プールで泳(およ)ぐことも好(す)きです。

My parents are much more into plants and gardening. My father is an expert with fish ponds and botanical gardens.

私(わたし)の両親(りょうしん)は、植物(しょくぶつ)やガーデニングにこだわっています。

父(ちち)は、魚(さかな)の池(いけ)とボタニカルガーデンのプロです。

If time and money allows, I love to travel as well. I already have been around Asia, mainly to Taiwan and to Macao in China. Anyway, having many hobbies and interests keep my mind active, and helps me to gain experience in life.

時間(じかん)とお金(かね)が許(ゆる)すかぎり、私(わたし)は旅行(りょこう)をしたいです。すでにアジア方面(ほうめん)、主(おも)に台湾(たいわ)やマカオを訪(おとず)れたことがあります。多(おお)くの趣味(しゅみ)と興味(きょうみ)を持(も)つことは、私(わたし)の心(こころ)を活発的(かっぱつてき)にさせ、人生(じんせい)での経験(けいけん)を豊富(ほうふ)にさせてくれます。

24. Studying Abroad

りゅうがく
留学

My name is Akio. I am from Okinawa and I would like to study in Germany.

私の名前はあきおです。沖縄出身で、将来はドイツで勉強をしたいと考えています。

I have excellent grades, but for admission to a German university, I'd need to speak sufficient German.

成績は大変いいのですが、ドイツの大学に入学するには、十分にドイツ語を話さなければなりません。

With a language exam, such as the DSH or TESTDAF I can prove my expertise.

DSHやTESTDといった言語テストで、ドイツ語の能力を証明することができます。

However, if I apply for an international major, a German language exam is not necessary. Then I am allowed to improve my German language skills in a regular language course.

けれども、国際的な分野を専攻すれば、ドイツ語のテストは必要なくなり、定期的にある言語のクラスでドイツ語のスキルを上げることができます。

Fortunately, I already speak some German.

幸い、私は少しだけドイツ語を話します。

25. A New Recipe
新しいレシピ

Molli is the owner of a small restaurant in a small town. She sells mainly fries and hamburgers.

モリーは小さな町にある小さなレストランを営んでいます。

彼女はおもに、フライドポテトとハンバーガーを売っています。

Most of the customers also like her food but some complain that the place is not clean and cockroaches running all over the place.

ほとんどのお客さんは彼女の料理を気に入っているのですが、

たまにレストランが汚れていてゴキブリが走り回っているので、不満を言っています。

Molli has plans to change her restaurant. It is going to be clean and offers healthy dishes.

モリーはレストランを変える計画をしています。きれいな場所で健康的

な料理を提供するのです。

Molli has bought a cookbook containing many Asian and diet recipes. Molli is inspired to change her menu.

彼女はアジアとダイエット料理がのっている本を買い、メニューを変更するためのアイ

ディアを得ました。

The following days Molli adds vegetable hamburgers to the menu. A customer asks what the hamburger is made of and Molli responds that it is made of bread and ground meat made of insects.

翌日、メニューに野菜ハンバーガーを追加しました。お客がこのハンバーガーは何から

できているのかを聞くと、モリーは、パンと虫のひき肉、と答えました。

She had prepared the ground meat herself, killing and using all the insects she can find in the restaurant.

彼女(かのじょ)はレストランにいるすべての虫(むし)を殺(ころ)して、そのひき肉(にく)を自分(じぶん)で準備(じゅんび)したのでした。

26. Social Media
ソーシャルメディア

My name is Nicole. The most important aspect of life to me is looking and feeling healthy. Being beautiful is also a part of my business.

私の名前はニコラです。私の人生の中で一番大切なことは、健康に気をつけることです。美しくなることも気にしていることの一つです。

A few years ago, I started an online business where I sell cosmetics and perfume.

数年前、コスメと香水のオンラインビジネスをはじめました。

To expand my business, I use different social media platforms to spread the message such as Twitter and Facebook.

ビジネスを大きくするため、ツイッターやフェイスブックなど、メッセージを拡散するためにいろいろなソーシャルメディアのプラットフォームを使っています。

Additionally, I use powerful visual social media; my favorites are Instagram and Pinterest.

さらに、私は有力なビジュアル型のソーシャルメディアも使っていて、その中でもお気に入りは、インスタグラムとピンタレストです。

I try to spread the word on how women can stay young and beautiful.

女性がどのようにして若さと美しさを保つのか、という内容のメッセージを広げようとしています。

Interestingly I receive a lot of new virtual friends, and it seems like everyone wants to connect with me.

おもしろいことに、私はバーチャルの友だちをたくさんつくることができました。みんなが、私とネット上でつながりたいようなのです。

In the end, many customers also become friends, or sometimes even business partners.

最終的には、多くの客と、ときにはビジネスパートナーとも友だちになることもあります。

I have never regretted going back to my old job as a sales clerk. My life, my friends, and my money are coming from my online business.

販売店員であった前の仕事に戻りたいとは決して思いません。私の人生、友だちそしてお金は全てオンラインビジネスにあるのです。

27. Vegan Food
ビーガンフード

Maria knows that she needs to stay on a diet. She has read many diet cookbooks and does stretching exercises in the morning hours.

マリアは、ダイエットをしなければならないと思っています。彼女は多くのダイエットの料理本を読み、朝の時間にはストレッチ体操をしています。

She also has studied and experimented with many diet recipes, but a lot of recipes contain meat which Maria tries to avoid.

ダイエットレシピの勉強をして実践しているのですが、多くのレシピには、マリアがさけようとしている肉類をふくんでいます。

However, cooking takes a lot of time and whenever possible she tries to find a healthy restaurant, as she doesn't want to cook every day.

料理には時間がかかるので、毎日料理をしたくないマリアは健康的なレストランを探しています。

A good friend of hers told her about a good vegetarian restaurant.

仲の良い彼女の友人がビーガンレストランをおすすめしてくれました。

Maria tries the restaurant and finds the dishes absolutely delicious.

マリアはそのレストランに行ってみたところ、とても美味しく感動しました。

Almost all of the dishes are vegetarian, and some are even only vegan.

ほとんど全ての料理がベジタリアンで、いくつかのものがビーガン料理でした。

After a short time, Maria has become a regular customer. Her favorite meal is vegetable soup which is supposed to have no meat at all.

それからしばらくして、マリアはそのレストランの常連になりました。彼女のお気に入りは、お肉が全く入っていないであろう野菜スープです。

One day she asks the cook why the soup is always so delicious, as she wants to know the secret.

ある日、彼女は秘密を知るため、なぜこのスープはこんなにおいしいのかを料理人に聞きました。

The cook answers that he is always using chicken stock.

彼は、チキンストックを使っているからだ、と答えたのでした。

28. Bad Luck
不幸(ふこう)

A Japanese man felt he was haunted by bad luck. Several times somebody had stolen food from his refrigerator at home.

ある日本人(にほんじん)の男性(だんせい)が不幸(ふこう)に見舞(みま)われました。誰(だれ)かが彼(かれ)の自宅(したく)にある冷蔵庫(れいぞうこ)から食(た)べ物(もの)をぬすんだのです。

That's why he eventually installed a security camera which would send images from his kitchen directly to his mobile phone.

なので、彼(かれ)はキッチンの写真(しゃしん)を携帯電話(けいたいでんわ)に直接送(ちょくせつおく)ることができるセキュリティカメラを設置(せっち)しました。

But instead of a burglar he discovered a stranger, who roamed in his house while he was absent.

けれども、不法侵入者(ふほうしんにゅうしゃ)のかわりに彼(かれ)が発見(はっけん)したのは、不在(ふざい)の間(あいだ)家(いえ)を歩(ある)き回(まわ)っている不思議(ふしぎ)な人物(じんぶつ)でした。

As soon as he saw this, he called the police.

それを見(み)るとすぐに彼(かれ)は警察(けいさつ)を呼(よ)びました。

They searched the house but nothing and nobody could be found.

警察(けいさつ)は彼(かれ)の家(いえ)を調(しら)べましたが、初(はじ)めは何(なに)も発見(はっけん)することができませんでした。

"We have seared all the places where someone could hide", the inspector remembered. "Then, when we opened a closet, there she was, hiding shivering in a corner we found this woman."

「私たちは、誰かが隠れていると疑われるすべての場所を見渡しました。」「そして、クローゼットの中を開けると、角で震えながら隠れている彼女がいたのです。」

She was identified as Tatsuko Horikawa, a homeless, who had been hiding in this house for almost one year, stealing food, taking showers and using the toilet.

彼女は ひろかわ とつこ という人物であると身元が特定されました。彼女はホームレスで、ほぼ1年前からその家に隠れながら、食べ物を盗み、シャワーを浴び、そしてトイレを使用していたのでした。

The 60 year old later told the police, she sneaked herself into the house when the owner forgot to lock the door.

60歳の警察官は、彼が鍵をかけ忘れたときに彼女が侵入したのだ、と言いました。

29. Our Hotel
私たちのホテル

We have just arrived at our hotel. This year we will spend our vacation in Spain.
私たちはホテルに着きました。今年は休暇をスペインで過ごします。

We have booked an all-inclusive hotel and the check-in was very efficient.
すべての設備が整ったホテルで、チェックインはとても簡単でした。

The friendly receptionist gave us the room key after we paid a security deposit.
セキュリティーのためのデポジットを支払った後、親切な受付の方が私たちに鍵を渡しました。

We are from England. At first, it seemed the hotel had a very high standard.
私たちはイギリスから来ました。はじめはかなり高級なホテルのように思えました。

The rooms were spacious and everything looked great.
部屋は広くて、すべてがよかったのです。

The next day things started to turn out different. We discovered fat cockroaches in the bathroom and the closets were dirty.
けれども次の日から、変化が起きました。私たちは太ったゴキブリをバスルームで発見し、そしてクローゼットが汚れていたことに気がつきました。

We bought travel insurance, but unfortunately they don't pay for dirty rooms.
私たちは旅行保険に加入していたのですが、汚れたホテルでの宿泊代の弁償には残念ながら適用されませんでした。

My husband had an idea. He took pictures of the closets and cockroaches.
そこで、私の夫があるアイディアを思いつきました。
彼はまずクローゼットとゴキブリの写真をとりました。

In a nearby pharmacy, we asked for medication against diarrhea.
次に、近くの薬局で、下痢止めの薬を購入しました。

I immediately contacted the insurance company and informed them that we have all become sick because of the unclean room.
そしてすぐ保険会社に部屋が清潔ではないために体調が悪くなってしまった、と連絡をしたのです。

I attached a photo of the medication and the receipt. A few weeks later the insurance had refunded our stay.
薬とレシートの写真も送りました。すると数週間後、保険会社は私たちの宿泊代を払い戻してくれたのです。

30. In the Theatre
映画館(えいがかん)で

This weekend the theatre is showing a truly interesting film. It's supposed to be a romantic movie. That's the reason I have invited a neighbour to accompany me, as she also likes romantic movies.

今週(こんしゅう)、映画館(えいがかん)でとてもおもしろそうな恋愛映画(れんあいえいが)が公開(こうかい)されます。なので、私(わたし)は恋愛映画(れんあいえいが)の好きな隣人(りんじん)をさそいました。

We buy popcorn and have a seat in the last row.
私(わたし)たちはポップコーンを買(か)って、最後列(さいこうれつ)に座(すわ)りました。

Actually, the movie has many romantic scenes with some of them being quite strong.
その映画(えいが)には、強(つよ)すぎるロマンスのシーンがいくつかありました。

The woman leans her head on my shoulder. I take her hand and let it rest on my lap.
彼女(かのじょ)は私(わたし)の肩(かた)に頭(あたま)を置(お)き、私(わたし)は彼女(かのじょ)の手(て)をとって私(わたし)の膝(ひざ)の上(うえ)に置(お)きました。

Suddenly the woman becomes angry, gets up, and leaves theatre.
すると突然(とつぜん)、彼女(かのじょ)は怒(おこ)って立(た)ち上(あ)がり、映画館(えいがかん)から出(で)て行(い)ったのです。

I smile and watch the rest of the movie. For me, it was a lovely evening.
私(わたし)は笑顔(えがお)でその映画(えいが)を最後(さいご)まで見続(みつづ)けました。私(わたし)にとっては、とても素敵(すてき)な夜(よる)でした

31. Dialogue - Where is our cat?

ダイアログ -私たちの猫はどこへ?

One morning we found a dead bird lying in front of our door. It looked like someone placed it there.

ある朝、死んだ鳥が誰かに置かれたように、私たちは家のドアの前に横たわっているのを見つけました。

I told my mother: "I think our cat Mika did this."

私は母に、「私たちのペットのミカがしたのよ。」と言いました。

My mother answered: "That's nature, we must not interfere."

すると母は、「自然とそこにあったのよ、あまり考えすぎないで。」と答えました。

I disagreed. "That's dangerous."

私は「それは危険よ。」と反対しました。

"Why?"
「どうして?」

"The dead bird carries bacteria. Mika will bring that bacteria into our house."

「死んだ鳥には菌があるのだから、ミカもそれを持って家に入っているかもしれない。」

"You are right", said my mother, concerned.

「そうね。」と母は理解しました。

My mother had to make a decision. She took the cat into the house.

母は決断し、猫を家に入れました。

After that I never saw Mika again.

その後、私がミカに再び会うことはありませんでした。

32. A special public swimming pool
特別な公共スイミングプール

Central Japan has mild winters, but In summertime Tokio can be very hot, and going to a public swimming pool is an excellent way to stay cool and fit.

日本の中心部の冬は穏やかですが、東京の夏はとても暑いです。なので、公共のスイミングプールで体を冷やすことが一番です。

Tokyo has no shortage of public swimming pools.

東京にはたくさんの公共のスイミングプールがあります。

Each has their own unique characteristics and above all provide the public with somewhere to cool down during the occasional heat wave of summer.

それぞれ特徴がありますが、すべての場所が猛暑の間、一般の人々に涼しい場所を提供しています。

The Tokyo Metropolitan Gymnasium is a public building so they offer swimming classes as well to the general public, it has a large number of facilities.

東京体育館は公共施設で、たくさんの設備があり、水泳の教室も行われています。

The good thing about this public facility is it opens early in the morning and closes quite late, weekdays at 11pm.

ここのよいところは、早朝から開き、平日だと午後11時と、比較的遅くに閉ることです。

However, they have some restrictions and you always have to wear a bathing cap.

けれども規制がいくつかあって、常に水泳帽をかぶらなければいけません。

33. On Fridays we go swimming
金曜日、水泳をしに行きます

We are a group of boys and are avid swimmers.
僕たちは、水泳に熱心な男子のグループです。

We are all foreigners in Japan, because our parents work here.
日本にいる外国人で、両親はこの国で働いています。

Most of us are twelve years old, and only our friend Peter is eleven.
ほとんどが12歳ですが、友人のピーターだけは17歳です。

Every Friday afternoon we go to the public swimming pool, the Metropolitan Gymnasium.
毎週金曜日の夕方、僕たちは公共のスイミングプールがある東京体育館に行きます。

First, we need to go to the locker rooms. There we change our clothing to proper swimmwear, and after that we'll take a shower.
まず、僕たちはローカールームに行って、水着に着替えます。その後、シャワーを浴びます。

Before and after swimming one has to take a shower, which is obligatory in public swimming pools.
水泳の前後には、シャワーを浴びなければならず、これは公共のスイミングプールにおいて、義務となっています。

Sometimes taking a shower takes quite some time, because we like to make jokes and are fooling around.

僕たちはときどき、ふざけながらシャワーを浴びるので時間がかかることがあります。

Once in the swimming pool, we jump from the plank and swim around.

スイミングプールに着くと、すぐさま飛び込み台からジャンプし、泳ぎます。

We start with 1000 feet breaststroke, after that, we usually go on to twenty minutes of freestyle. Towards the end we just play water ball.

まず1000フィートの平泳ぎから始め、次に20分間フリースタイルで泳ぎます。最後は、水球をします。

At the edge of the pool a lifeguard is always there observing us.

プールの端では、常に見張り人が僕たちを監視しています。

Last week when we were finished swimming, we didn't shower afterwards because an unknown child had left his excrements in the shower.

先週、水泳をし終わった後、シャワー室に子どもが排便をしていたのを見つけたので、僕たちはシャワーを浴びませんでした。

34. The Experiment
実験(じっけん)

At school, Sandra asks her classmates: "Is it true that old people smell different?"
学校(がっこう)で、サンドラはクラスメイトに、「お年寄(としよ)りの匂(にお)いが違(ちが)うのは本当(ほんとう)?」と聞(き)きました。

Her friend Gabi replies, "Well, they all smell rotten."
彼女(かのじょ)の友(とも)だちであるガビは、「そうよ、みんな腐(くさ)った匂(にお)いがするのよ。」と答(こた)えました。

John laughs. "No, only the dead are rotten. Old people are not dead yet. They are still alive."
ジョンは、「違(ちが)う。死(し)んだ人間(にんげん)だけ腐(くさ)った匂(にお)いがするんだ。お年寄(としよ)りはまだ死(し)んでない生(い)きているよ。」と笑(わら)いました。

Gabi chuckles. "All right. Then we will call them mature. But as a matter of fact, I don't care how we call old people. I just don't want to be near them."
ガビは「そうね。彼(かれ)らは成熟(せいじゅく)しているのね。でも実際(じっさい)のところ、お年寄(としよ)りをどう呼(よ)ぶかには興味(きょうみ)はなくて、私(わたし)はただ近寄(ちかよ)りたくないの。」とくすくす笑(わら)いました。

John raises his hand. "Wait a minute. I once saw an experiment on YouTube. It shows that old people don't smell any different.
ジョンは手(て)をあげ、「ちょっと待(ま)って。Youtubeでお年寄(としよ)りの匂(にお)いに違(ちが)いはないと証明(しょうめい)しているある実験(じっけん)を見(み)たことがあるよ。

Scientists let three groups of people sleep in shirts: old, middle-aged, and young. Each person had to sleep in the same shirt for five nights, and the shirts were not washed.

科学者が、お年寄り、中年、若者と3つのグループに分けて、5日間夜に同じシャツを着て寝かせたんだ。そして、そのシャツは洗わないままでね。

Then they asked volunteers to smell the shirts.

そして、ボランティアの人たちにその匂いをかいでもらったんだ。

The volunteers didn't know which shirt came from what group, but all agreed said that the shirts of the old people smelled the best. "

すると、多くの人が匂いの違いがわからないけれども、一番お年寄りが着ていたシャツの匂いが良いと答えたんだ。」と説明しました。

"What kind of volunteers were these people who want to smell old people's shirts?" asks Sandra.

サンドラは、「そのシャツの匂いを嗅いだボランティアの人々はどんな人たちだったの？」と聞きました。

35.Best Friends
親友

Since I was going to school, Anna has been my best friend. We were about eleven years old when we first met.

学生のころから、アンナは私の親友です。初めて出会ったときは11歳でした。

Even though she lives now in Japan, we have always maintained good contact. We regularly talk on the internet via services such as Skype.

今彼女は日本に住んでいますが、私たちは連絡をとりあっています。スカイプのようなインターネットサービスでよく話をします。

we have always supported each other even when one of us was in trouble.

私たちは、どちらか片方に問題が起きたとしても、お互い支え合っています。

I always have been good with languages while my friend is good with literature. Anna has always helped me with my research and I helped her with learning Japanese.

私は言語が、アンナは文学が得意です。彼女が私のリサーチを手伝い、

私は彼女に日本語を教えます。

As teenagers we often consulted each other about women issues and boys.

10代のときにはよく、女子の問題や男の子について話しました。

Our friendship has helped both of us, but especially Anna. When you live abroad you need all the help you can get.

特にアンナとのフレンドシップはお互いを助けあっている関係です。海外に住んでいると、たくさんの助けが必要となります。

36. The Order
オーダー

A couple from Ohio is on vacation in Miami. They are sitting at a beach side restaurant and are ready to order.

オハイオから来たあるカップルは現在、バカンスをマイマミで過ごしています。彼らは、海沿いのレストランの席に座り、注文するのを待っています。

Finally, the waiter comes. He brings two menu cards and then disappears. The couple looks at the menu and is not impressed.

ついに、ウェイターがやって来て、メニューを2つ渡し去って行きました。カップルはあまりうれしそうで はない様子でメニューを見ています。

There the man discovers dried-up Ketchup remains on the menu and shakes it with disgust.

男性は、メニューにケチャップの汚れがあるのを見つけ、不愉快に思っていました。

The waiter takes his time to serve other guests first and finally returns to the table with two glasses and water.

ウェイターは他のお客にサービスをした後、ようやくグラス2つとお水をもって戻ってきました。

He holds the glasses with his fingers on the edges, puts them on the table and disappears again.

彼はグラスの口元をもち、それらを机の上において再び去っていきました。

The woman says to her husband. "I can see his fingerprints on the glasses. That's disgusting. Can you tell the waiter to bring us two other glasses?"

女性は夫に、「グラスに指紋がある。とても不愉快だから、新しいグラスを持ってきてもらうようウエイターに頼んでくれる？」と言いました。

"But then the waiter wants to know why and we would have a serious discussion."

夫は「けれども、ウエイターは理由を知りたがるだろうし、そうすると口論になるかもしれない。」と答えました。

"Then ask him if he can bring us two closed water bottles."

「では、ボトルで閉まった水をもってきてもらうように頼んで。」と妻が言いました。

"For that we would need to pay extra. But I have an idea; I think we still have water bottles in the car. I'm going to get them."

「それだと無料ではなくなる。でもいいアイディアがあるよ。車に水のボトルがまだあったでしょう。それをもってくるよ。」と夫。

"Good Idea. Please also bring the soap and a cloth so we can clean up the table before the waiter returns."

「いいアイディアね。それと、ウエイターが戻ってくる前にテーブルをきれいにできるよう、ソープと布巾をもってきてちょうだい。」

37. Food Poisoning
食中毒

Me and my brother Marc are visiting Japan, and today he feels terrible; he's been in bed since yesterday.

私と弟のマークは日本を訪れているのですが、今日彼の調子が良さそうではありません。

He has nausea, a headache, coughing and diarrhea. He also feels extremely exhausted and tired.

昨日からずっとベットにいます。症状は、吐き気、頭痛、せき、そして下痢で、すごく疲れているようです。

I know a little about diseases and figure from his conditions that he has food poisoning.

私は病気について少し知っているので、彼の状態からみて、食中毒であると判断しました。

It's a dangerous situation, because Marc is already dehydrated!

マークはすでに脱水症状を起こしてるのでとても危険な状況です。

I recommend my brother to stay in bed and take strong medication which I buy in a pharmacy.

私は、薬局で買った効き目のある薬を飲んで、ベットで休むようにすすめました。

My brother believes his food poisoning comes from a Madagasca cockroach sushi he had eaten the day before at a eating party.

弟は、食中毒はパーティーの前日に食べたマダダスカの寿司が原因だろう、と思っています。

38. New Year's Eve in Europe
ヨーロッパのニューイヤーズ・イブ

Many traditional events of the Japanese New Year are still celebrated on the first day of the year.

日本では、新年を祝う伝統的な行事の多くが、新年の最初の日に行われます。

New Year's Eve is always the night of December 31st in Germany, France and Italy.

ドイツやフランス、イタリアでは、大晦日はつねに12月31日の夜です。

Most people celebrate New Year's Eve with friends and family. At midnight there are always fireworks.

ほとんどの人たちが、友だちや家族とともにその日を祝います。真夜中には花火が打ち上げられます。

Most families also prepare a special meal. A typical New Year's meal in Europe is carp, goose, or hotdogs.

そして家族は特別な料理を準備します。ヨーロッパでの代表的な新年の料理は、鯉、ガチョウなどを使ったものです。

Often, New Year's Eve is an occasion for many people to drink lots of alcohol. Most young people also go to parties, and some even go dancing!

ニューイヤーズ・イブはたくさんのお酒を飲む機会があって、若者たちはパーティーやクラブに行ってダンスをします！

January 1st is a holiday all over the continent, with almost all businesses closed. On the 2nd of January however, it's a normal working day in Europe.

1月1日には、どこもかしこも休暇で、ほどんどのお店が閉まっていますが、1月2日は普通の日なので、人々は働いています。

39. The Circus
サーカス

Today I went with my mother to the circus. The show started at six, but we arrived early because we knew there would be a long line at the ticket box.

今日、私は母とサーカスを見に行きました。ショーは18時に始まるのですが、私たちはチケット売場のところに行列があることを考えて、早めに到着しました。

My mother asked why the tickets are so expensive.

チケット売場で私の母はチケットがなぜこんなに高いのか質問しました。

The salesperson explained that they have big animals such as tigers, etc. and they need to eat enormous amounts of meat every day.

すると、販売員の人は、ショーにはトラのような大量の肉を毎日食べる大きな動物がいて、そのエサ代をおぎなう必要があるからだ、と説明しました。

Finally, the show starts.

やがて、ショーが始まりました。

First we see a clown who makes jokes by gesturing with his hands.

最初に、道化師が手を使ってジェスチャーをしながらギャグをしました。

Then a huge cage is set up and the animals arrive. We see an elephant that raises a leg, a monkey that is dressed in a girly school costume, and then we see the big cats led into the cage.

それから大きなケージが置かれ、動物たちが登場しました。象が足を上げたり、さるが

女子学生の格好をしていたりしていました。

そして、大きなネコ科の動物たちはケージの中に入っていきました。

A tiger has to jump through a burning ring, and a lion has to jump from stool to stool.

とらは 火の輪を飛び越え、ライオンはいすからいすへ飛び渡っていました。

I ask my mother if the animals are also doing such things in nature. My mother responds that she doesn't know.

私は母に、動物たちは自然の中でもこのようなことをしているのか聞きました。すると

母は、わからない、と答えました。

40. The Car Accident
車の事故

Last month I drove home from work just as I do every day.
先月のことですが、私はいつものように仕事から自宅まで車で帰っていました。

I was driving slowly and stopped at a traffic light. Suddenly, I heard a loud bang.
ゆっくりと運転して、信号のところで止まりました。すると突然、私は大きな物音を聞きました。

The car behind me had hit my bumper.
後ろにいた車が私のバンパーにぶつかってきたのです。

I immediately got out of the car and saw that the taillight was broken.
私はすぐさま車の外へ出て、テールライトが壊れているのを見ました。

The driver admitted his guilt immediately and offered me money for the damage. He wanted to give me five hundred dollars cash.
私の車にぶつかってきた運転手は、自身のしたことを認め、壊した代わりに現金で＄500を私に渡したいと言いました。

I rejected his offer and told him I was going to call the police.
けれども私は彼の提案をことわり、今から警察を呼ぶと伝えました。

Suddenly all around me went black.

すると急に視界が暗くなりました。

I have no memory what happened at that moment. I awoke in a hospital. The doctor told me somebody had shot me from behind.

その後の記憶はなく、気がついたときには私は病院にいました。医者はだれかに後ろから殴られたのだ、と教えてくれました。

41. A Japanese in Munich
ミュンヘンの日本人

Taro is Japanese. He has traveled to Germany many times, because he was studying there.

たいとは日本人です。彼はドイツで勉強をしていてるので、何度もドイツ国内を旅行しました。

Taro appreciates the German culture and customs. Tidiness, and interests in all technical things are important to him, because these things remind him on his own country.

ドイツの文化や習慣を彼はとても気に入っています。例えば、清潔さ、テクノロジー分野への関心は彼の母国を思い出させます。

Taro is especially fond of Munich with its traditions and especially its beer culture. He loves the Hofbräuhaus which is probably the most famous beer house in Germany.

特にミュンヘンには伝統とビールの文化があるので彼のお気に入りの場所です。おそらくドイツで一番有名であろうホフブロイハウスが、彼は大好きです。

It is not even midday when he enters the Hofbrauhaus. There are no guests, except one old man who sits in the corner and drinks beer.

ホフブロイハウスに入ったときは、まだ正午でした。角の席にすわりビールを飲んでいる老人をのぞくと、客はまだいません。

Taro just takes a seat in front of old the man and orders a beer for himself. Tairo smiles at the old man.

たいとはその老人（ろうじん）の前（まえ）にすわり、ビールを注文（ちゅうもん）しました。そして男性（だんせい）に微笑（ほほえ）みかけました。

"Do you mind if I join you?"

「一緒（いっしょ）に飲（の）んでもいいですか？」

The old man nods.

老人（ろうじん）はうなずきました。

Tairo asks. "If I may ask, why do you like beer?"

たいとはたずねます。「どうしてビールが好（す）きなのですか？」

The old man looks up and smiles. "Because, I am a real Bavarian from Munich".

老人（ろうじん）は顔（かお）を上（あ）げ笑顔（えがお）で、「私（わたし）はミュンヘンのバイエルン人（じん）だからだよ。」と答（こた）えました。

Taro keeps smiling. "Munich is such a beautiful city."

たいとも続（つづ）けて笑顔（えがお）で言（い）います。「ミュンヘンはとてもきれいな街（まち）ですね。」

The old man takes a sip of his beer. "I have not seen much of the city recently."
老人はビールを一口飲みました。「最近は街をよく見てないんだ。」

"Is this your favourite beer house?"
「ここはお気に入りのビアハウスですか？」

"I know this beer house very well", replies the old man.
「ここのことはよく知っているよ。」と老人は答えます。

Taro wonders. "Excuse me for asking, but how old are you?"
たいとはすこし戸惑いながら、「失礼ですが、おいくつですか？」とたずねました。

"Soon I will be soon one hundred years old", replies the old man.
「もうすぐ、100歳になるよ。」

Taro shakes his head. "Unbelievable. Do you live in Munich?"
「信じられない。あなたはミュンヘンに住んでいるのですか？」

"I live right here in the basement of the Hofbräuhaus", answers the man.
「私は、ホフブロイハウスの地下に住んでいるんだ。」

Taio shakes his head". Since when are you living here?

たいとは頭(あたま)をふります。「いつからですか？」

"I am hiding here. I have never left this beer house since the end of hostilities in 1945."

「1945年(ねん)の終戦(しゅうせん)の後(あと)からずっとホフブロイハウスを離(はな)れたことがない。ここに隠(かく)れているんだ。」と老人(ろうじん)は答(こた)えました。

Part 2 Japanese Short Stories for intermediate students including Hiragana, Kanji and Furigana

42. A Special Cooking Course

特別（とくべつ）なクッキングコース

My wife and I spent last year on one of the new cruise lines around the southern half of Japan.

去年（きょねん）、私（わたくし）の妻（つま）と私（わたくし）は、日本（にほん）の南側（みなみがわ）を巡（めぐ）る新（あたら）しいクルーズ船（ふね）の1つで過（す）ごしました。

It was upon the Merry Princess, a 2,500-passenger behemoth that contained every luxury and distraction that a modern man could possibly crave.

それは、現代（げんだい）の男性（だんせい）が羨（うらや）むであろう贅沢（ぜいたく）と娯楽（ごらく）を有（ゆう）し、2500人（にん）の乗客（じょうきゃく）を抱（かか）える巨大（きょだい）なクルーズ船（せん）である、メリープリンセスでした。

We both found it to be a relaxing, easy and relatively inexpensive way to explore some of the more "off-the-beaten-path" areas of the country.

私（わたくし）たちは、この船旅（ふなたび）は落（お）ち着（つ）いてかつゆったりしていると思（おも）いました。そして、その国（くに）の"普通（ふつう）ではない"場所（ばしょ）を見（み）る方法（ほうほう）としては比較的安（ひかくてきやす）いでしょう。

We were having a grand time, and we both experienced the peace of mind that comes from untethering yourself from the troubles of daily life.

私たちはすてきな時間を過ごし、日々のトラブルから解放することにより心が休まりました。

That is why I was so shocked to one day wake up and find myself in a hospital bed.

だからこそ、私はある日目が覚めて、病院のベッドの上にいることに気づいた時とてもショックでした。

It was certainly not the way I had envisioned ending our cruise.

私たちのクルーズ船の旅は、このような結末になるはずではありませんでした。

We stopped in Beppu, a spa town designed for tourists and built over an active geothermal area.

私たちは別府に停留しました。別府は旅行客のために計画された温泉街であり、活発な地熱地帯で構築されました。

This feature afforded the town nine small clusters of hot springs and geysers known, somewhat cheekily, as "The Hells".

この温泉街の特徴は温泉と間欠泉で構成される9つの小さな集団で、やや大げさです が"地獄"として知られています。

English was not widely spoken here and the signs about the town were just an undiscernible jumble of Japanese kanji.

そこでは、あまり英語が通じず、町の標識にはゴチャゴチャしていて見分けにくい 日本語の漢字が書かれていました。

To find oneself without bearings, that is the mark of true adventure, or at least that is what I tried to tell myself at the time.

自分自身で迷うことは真の探検の象徴、もしくはそれは少なくとも当時私が 自分自身に伝えようとしたことでした。

We dipped our toes into the culture without putting our *entire* foot in, and I think we were all the happier for it.

私_{わたくし}たちは、足全体_{あしぜんたい}ではなくつま先_{さき}だけをその文化_{ぶんか}に浸_{ひた}すだけで満足_{まんぞく}していました。

My wife already knew a little about the local culture, so she helped me when I was most ill at ease.

私_{わたくし}の妻_{つま}は、日本文化_{にほんぶんか}について少_{すこ}しだけ知_しっていたので、私_{わたくし}がすごく不安_{ふあん}に思_{おも}った時_{とき}に助_{たす}けてくれました。

One of the activities we chose was a cooking course conducted in one of the many beautiful parks around Beppu.

たくさんあるアクティビティーの中_{なか}から、私_{わたくし}たちは別府市_{べっぷし}の近_{ちか}くにある美_{うつく}しい公園_{こうえん}の1つで行_{おこな}われたクッキングコースを選_{えら}びました。

I already knew a thing or two about Japanese cooking and cuisine, but I was far from being a pro.

私_{わたくし}は、日本料理_{にほんりょうり}について1つあるいは2つのことを知_しっていましたが、プロとは程遠_{ほどとお}かったです。

I've never been a fan of sushi nor shabu-shabu, and I generally prefer my Asian food to be of the shopping mall variety.

私は、寿司もしくはシャブシャブが好きではなく、普段はショッピングモールにある

様々なアジア料理を好みます。

But I wanted to humor my wife so I agreed to take part in the course.

しかし、私は妻の機嫌をとりたかったため、そのコースに参加することにしました。

The instructor was an elderly man who was so short that he had to stand on a box to see over the "etsubin", a Japanese term for a cast iron kettle used for boiling water.

講師の人は年配の男性でしたが、彼はとても背が低かったため箱の上に立って、湯を沸かすための日本の鉄製のやかんである"鉄瓶"越しで見渡さなければなりませんでした。

This one in front of him was huge, nearly a yard across and heated from hot stones pulled from the nearby springs.

彼の前にあるそれは大きく、約1ヤードの大きさで、近くの温泉から取り出された熱い石で熱せられました。

To our disgust, he threw living frogs into the open kettle, where they crashed into the water with a great *hiss* and sizzle.

不快なことに、彼は生きているカエルを蓋がされていないやかんに入れ、その途端シューシューという大きな音が鳴りました。

Frogs have always been one of my favorite animals, and I treat them with a kind of reverence they may not even deserve.

カエルは私の好きな動物の一つで、彼らにふさわしいものではないかもしれませんが、私は彼らにある種の尊敬の念をもって接していました。

But I felt that I had to protest this cruel behavior.

しかし、私はその残酷な行動に抗うべきだと思いました。

I stepped forward and shouted at him like a drunken sailor, loud and obnoxiously so that he would surely get my message.

私は前に出て、彼に聞こえるように、酔っぱらった水兵のように声高にかつ口汚く彼に向かって叫びました。

"Hey man, what do you think you are doing!?

"おい！何をやっているのかわかっているのですか！？

At least kill those frogs in a humane way.

少なくとも人道的な方法でそれらのカエルを殺すべきです。

Don't just toss them into boiling water like their lives are of so little value!"

彼らの命を尊重せずに、沸いている水に投げ入れるべきではないです！"

My wife pulled me aside and explained to me that one of the rules of this culture was never to disagree with your elders in a public setting, such as a meeting or a group course like the one we were partaking in.

妻は私を脇に引っ張り、日本文化では会議や私たちが参加しているようなグループコースなどの公の場で、年上の人に逆らってはいけないのだと私に説明しました。

She told me that I was doing the instructor a grave disservice and that I was causing him to "lose face", something they call "mentsu wo ushinau".

彼女は、その講師にとってはひどい仕打ちであり、私は彼の"顔をつぶす"つまり彼の"面子を失わせる"ことをしてしまったと言いました。

I looked at the little old man and saw him scowling at me, his face turning a deep purple under his kasa.

私がその背の低い男を見ると、彼は怖い顔をしてこちらを見ており、また彼の顔は笠の下で濃い紫色に変わっていました。

But this did not matter to me at the time.

しかし、その時私は気にしませんでした。

I was so taken aback by his treatment of the frogs that I was blinded by rage; all custom and delicacy was thrown to the wind.

私は、彼のそのカエルの扱いに驚き、また怒りで礼儀や気遣いを忘れ周囲が見えなくなっていました。

I pointed my finger at him and explained that animal cruelty was something I simply could not let go.

私は彼の方へ指を差し、動物虐待は許されないことだと説明しました。

"End this show right now! This…this…spectacle!"

"この見世物を終わらせてくれ！この…この…ショーを！"

Unexpectedly, he came forward and jabbed a finger into my chest and told me that "we are still in Japanese territory" or something of the like.

思いもよらず、彼は前に出て指で私の胸を突き"私たちはまだ日本にいる"といったようなこと言いました。

My wife then whispered into my ear that he had challenged me; I guessed he wanted me to show the audience a real alternative to the process he adhered to.

妻は私の耳元で、彼は私を挑発していると囁き、私は、彼は私に周りの人々に彼のその行為に替わるものを見せて欲しいのではないかと思いました。

I saw him standing there, now with a smug smile spreading across his face, motioning me towards the box where he had been presiding over the boiling cauldron.

彼はそこに立ち、顔には得意げな笑みを浮かべ、沸騰している大釜越しで講義をしていたその箱に来るよう私に合図をしました。

He gestured again and suddenly I became unsure of myself.

彼は再び同じ合図をしましたが、私は突然自信を持てなくなりました。

I had never cooked frogs in my life.

私は今までカエルを料理したことがありません。

But I decided to show some courage and approached the wooden platform.

しかし、私はいくらかの勇気を見せることを決め、木製の演台へと近づいていきました。

I would end this spectacle on my own terms.

私は私自身でこのショーを終わらせることでしょう。

The people around us, the tourists and growing crowd of locals alike, applauded, curiosity plainly written on their faces.

私たちの周囲にいた観光客や地元の人々は、拍手を送り、彼らの顔は好奇心あふれる顔でした。

When I stepped up onto the box and looked out onto the crowd, I was quite at a loss about what to do.

私がその箱の上に上がって群集を見た時、何をするべきなのか困ってしまいました。

I didn't have the heart to kill these frogs, no matter the method.

どのような手段を使ったとしても、私はこれらのカエルを殺す気などありませんでした。

So in the end, I decided that the best course of action was just to take the bag with the frogs away.

結局、とるべき行動はカエルを鞄に入れて持ち去ることだと思いました。

That way, they could live a happy life amongst the puddles and rotten drainage.

そうすれば、カエルは水たまりや腐食した排水管で幸せな日々を送るでしょう

At least I would end this cruel charade!

少なくとも、私はこの残酷なゲームを終わらせるでしょう！

I started to gather all the frogs and place them tenderly in the bag, for I did not want to crush any of them in my haste.

私は全てのカエルを集め始め、傷つけないようにそっと鞄の中に入れました。

I was about to make a break for it, when I was suddenly pushed from behind.

突然後ろから押された時、危うくカエルを傷つけることころでした。

I fell forward and before I knew it, my entire being was awash in blinding pain.

私は、気づく前に前方に倒れ、全身がひどい痛みであふれていました。

Heat enveloped me; I felt it sear my bones.

私の体は熱さで覆われ、骨は焼け焦がれたような感覚でした。

I passed out.

そして、私は気絶しました。

When I came to, I was in the hospital that I mentioned at the beginning of this tale.

意識が戻った時、このお話の冒頭で述べたように私は病院の中にいました。

The sterile surroundings confused me; I was awash in hard, white light.

無菌環境に戸惑い、私は白い光にさらされていました。

I quickly noticed that my legs and feet were wrapped entirely in bandages.

すぐに、私の両足全体が包帯で巻かれていることに気づきました。

I looked at my arms: the surface of my skin looked like dirty, pinkish crushed stone.

自分の腕を見ると、皮膚は汚いように見え、石でぶつけたかのようにピンクがかっていました。

Later, the Japanese doctor teasingly scolded me.

後に、日本人の医者はからかうように私を叱りました。

"Mister, this is what you get for causing someone to lose face.

"ご主人、他人の面子をつぶすとこうなるのです。

You have only been boiled alive."

あなたは生きたまま煮られただけです。"

43. Nagano Gold
長野(ながの)の金(きん)

A good friend of mine was getting married, and what's more, he had chosen to hold the ceremony in the heart of the Nagano Basin, somewhere west of Tokyo.

私(わたくし)の親友(しんゆう)が結婚(けっこん)しようとしており、その上(うえ)、式(しき)を東京(とうきょう)の西側(にしがわ)にある長野県(ながのけん)の盆地(ぼんち)の中心(ちゅうしん)で挙(あ)げることにしました。

Naturally, I was invited because we had been buddies ever since my junior year at college.

私(わたくし)と彼(かれ)は大学時代(だいがくじだい)以来(いらい)からの友人同士(ゆうじんどうし)なので、当然私(とうぜんわたくし)も招待(しょうたい)されました。

And what a wedding it turned out to be.

そして、それはすごい結婚式(けっこんしき)でした。

He was never one to lack for extravagance, he even rented a trio of Japanese clowns, *poirots* as the locals would say, who had every guest reeling with laughter, and the cake was a multi-tiered, lavish affair that was as beautiful looking as it was tasting.

彼はかなりのお金を使いました。地元でポワロズと呼ばれている日本人の3人組のピエロを呼びゲストを笑わせ、ケーキは多層で豪華であるだけでなく美味しかったです。

After the wedding concluded, my partner and I, someone who I had only recently started dating, decided to stick around for a few days and check out all the local attractions.

結婚式後、私と最近付き合い始めたパートナーは、一緒に数日間その辺りをブラブラして、そこにある地元のアトラクションで遊びました。

We took a public minibus into the wilds about Nagano, and honestly,, there is no prettier nature to be found in the whole wide world.

私たちは、公共のマイクロバスに乗って長野の自然を見ましたが、正直言って、ここより素晴らしい自然はどこにもないでしょう。

Surrounding you are mountains, frothing rivers, and a variety of mountain-flowers which I had never seen before.

そこには、山、泡立つ川、山にある今まで見たことのない様々な花がありました。

The first day of our excursion we explored the riverbeds, where boulders strewn about liberally contain fantastic minerals in a variety of colors.

小旅行の1日目、私たちは、幻想的で様々な色の鉱物を含んでいる大きな石があちらこちらにある川床を探索しました。

The air was crisp and fresh, and the river was made of snowmelt water; you could literally *smell* the ancient ice on the wind, a smell that brought me to another time and place.

空気は心地よくかつ新鮮でした。川の水は雪解け水で、文字通り風に吹かれる古代の氷の匂いがし、私を別の時間と場所へ連れてくれて行ってくれるかのようでした。

The best part about it, you didn't have to spend a cent up here, unlike the resort towns we were used to.

最も素晴らしかったのは、私たちがいた観光都市と違って1セントも消費する必要がなかったということです。

Everything was free, the glorious bounty of mother nature.

壮大な母なる自然の恵みのすべてが無料でした。

The following day made an even greater impression.

次の日はさらに素晴らしかったです。

We trekked on over to KomakeDake, a peak located in the Central Alps that measures nearly 2600 meters.

私たちは、山頂が中央アルプスに位置する約2600メートルの駒ヶ岳へ向かいました。

We took a bus and then a fast-moving cable car to the KomakeDake lookout, which afforded us a view over all that wild expanse.

バスで向かい、高速ケーブルカーに乗り継いだ後に駒ヶ岳展望台に到着し、そこで

私たちは広々とした自然を見渡しました。

We attempted a bit of hiking and due to the great weather were able to see over the Northern Japanese Alps, an experience that will never leave me.

私たちはハイキングを少し試みたところ、天気が良かったので日本の北アルプスを

見渡せました。私にとって忘れ難い経験となりました。

We decided to descend by foot, which we were told would take roughly six hours if one's constitution was up to snuff.

歩いて山を下ろうとしましたが、体調が悪くなければ大体6時間かかると言われました。

As we were making our way down, a Japanese tour guide suddenly appeared out of the blue.

私たちが山を下っていると、突然日本人ツアーガイドが現れました。

He was dressed strangely, in what looked like an ancient kimono, though it was considerably soiled.

彼の服装は、昔の着物のような感じの奇妙なものでしたが、かなり汚れていました。

He told us that for a small fee he would show us a path that was both easier and more enjoyable.

彼は、安い料金でもっと歩きやすくて楽しい道を教えてあげると言いました。

When I told him that we were quite content with our current route, he kept pressing us with assurances that it would be "healthier for us" to take the path that he had in mind.

私が彼に今の道ですごく満足していると言ったら、彼は彼がすすめたその道の方が"私たちにとってもっと健康的"だと主張し続けました。

Just when I was on the verge of telling him *No* for the final time, my partner saw something glittering in the nearby streambed, just where the water was pooled, making it calm and clear.

私が断ろうとした時、私のパートナーが川床の近くで何か光るものを見ました。

そこにはちょうど水がたまっていて、そのため静かできれいな場所でした。

We made our way over to the water's edge and started searching the sandy bed just below the surface.

私たちはその水の端へ行き、水面のすぐ下の砂のベッドを探し始めました。

Suddenly, my partner screeched in excitement.

突然、パートナーは興奮して甲高い声を発しました。

He lifted his hand clear of the water and showed me its contents: a solid chunk of gold, or at least what looked like gold.

彼は、手を水から離し、その手の中を見せてくれました。そこには固い金の塊あるいは少なくとも金のようなものがありました。

It shone warmly in the alpine sun, so bright that I thought it too good to be true.

それはアルプスの日光で暖かく輝いており、出来すぎた話だと思いました。

We were so overcome with excitement that we forgot about the tour guide that had just so recently badgered us about the alternative path.

私たちは、興奮のあまり別の道をしつこくすすめてきたツアーガイドのことをすっかり忘れていました。

We hastily made our way down the mountain via the original, well-trodden path, and as soon as we reached the town, went straight to the closest exchange shop known to trade in gold.

私たちは、道を変えずに急いで山を下り、町に着いたら金を換金してくれる両替店へすぐに向かいました。

Behind the counter was a lean Japanese man with a serious expression and cold demeanor, and when we broached the topic of selling him gold, he grew plainly suspicious, but his English was quite good.

カウンターの向こうには1人の日本人男性が真剣な表情と冷たい態度でもたれており、金を売りたいと言ったら疑ってきましたが、彼の英語は非常に上手でした。

"I need to ask you. Where do you find this gold?"

"聞きたいことがあります。どこでこの金を手に入れましたか？"

"Well, we found it somewhere, can't say for sure where it was."

"まあ、見つけた場所についてはっきりと言えません。"

He insisted: "Did you find it up on the mountain?"

さらに彼は、"これを山で見つけましたか？"と聞きました。

He continued to explain that if we *had* found the gold somewhere on the mountainside, we should buy some proper equipment and continue prospecting, for we must have had natural luck concerning these things.

彼は続けて、私たちがその金を山腹で見つけたのであれば、適切な道具を買って金を探した方がいいと言いました。私たちは運が良かったのでしょう。

He even ventured to say that he had equipment available, though it came with a price.

さらに、彼は思い切って無料ではないけれどその道具を貸せますと言いました。

That night, in our hotel suite, we couldn't sleep a lick.

その夜、私たちはホテルのスイートルームで少しも眠ることができませんでした。

We were up all night trying to decide what to do next.

私たちは、一晩中次に何をすべきか考えていました。

We were scheduled to go home the next day, but should we not stay longer?

次の日に自宅へ帰る予定でしたが、もっと長く滞在するべきなのでしょうか？

Should we try to change our travel plans, call our respective jobs, ask for more time off?

職場に電話をして、休暇の延長をお願いするべきなのでしょうか？

What if there was more than just one nugget, perhaps an entire lode?

そこにもっと金の塊があるか金脈があったらどうしましょうか？

We thought we could be missing out on a once in a lifetime opportunity if we did not at least go back and check it out.

私たちは、少なともその場所へ行って確認しなければ、一生に一度のチャンスを逃すかもしれないと思いました。

We made our decision.

私たちは決断しました。

The next morning, after paying a somewhat exuberant price to rent prospecting equipment, we tried to find the same path that had led us to the pool which we had by now begun calling *our little spot*.

次の日の朝、探索のための道具のレンタル料金を払い、同じ道を通って再びあの私たちの小さな場所へと向かいました。

By late afternoon, exhausted and weary from the climb, we finally reached the selfsame spot.

夕方近くになり、私たちは山登りで疲れながらも、ついにその場所に着きました。

And like before, we immediately saw something shining just below the water's surface.

以前と同じように、水面のすぐ下に光っているものが見えました。

In fact, the entire creek bed was aglitter, for there must have been thousands of small pieces sparkling intensely, practically offering themselves to our greedy hands.

事実、川床全体は輝いており、たくさんの激しい輝きが私たちの欲張りな手によって拾われるのです。

We filled our backpacks and pockets with as much as we possibly could, and so burdened made our way back to civilization.

私たちは、それらをバックパックとポケットに出来る限りたくさん詰め、戻っていきました。

Just before nightfall we reached the village, whose margins were made up of tightly clustered ramshackle dwellings.

ちょうど日暮れ前、私たちはある村につき、その村の端にはぼろ家で敷き詰められていました。

The man who worked the exchange shop was standing in the doorway, almost as if he had been expecting us at that very moment.

両替店の男性が出入り口に立っており、まさにこの瞬間を待っていたかのようでした。

He smiled, and it was a smile full of knowing.

彼は何か知っているかのように微笑みました。

"Good evening, were you lucky again?"

"こんばんは、また見つかりましたか？"

My partner pulled a good-sized nugget from his pocket and proudly displayed it to the shopkeeper.

私のパートナーは、ちょうどいいサイズの塊をポケットから出し、それを誇らしげにその店主に見せました。

"You could say we were lucky again.

"また運がよかったとえるでしょう。

Probably more than lucky."

たぶんそれ以上ですね。"

At this point the shopkeeper produced a small dictionary from his back pocket.

この時、店主は後ポケットから小さな辞書を取り出しました。

"My friends, there is an English word for it.

"それを表現するある英語の言葉があります。

If I can just find it…oh, here it is."

見つかるといいのですが...あ、ここにありました。"

I made to look at the dictionary, but he pulled it away from my grasp and puffed himself up as if about to deliver an important speech.

私はその辞書を覗き込みましたが、彼は引き離しまるで重要なスピーチをするかのように得意になりました。

"This is called *Fool's* Gold.

"これは愚か者の金と呼ばれています。

There is a Japanese saying which I think is appropriate: if you believe in something that you wish to be true, then what's called for is hard work.

これにふさわしい日本のことわざがあります。真実だろうと思っているものがあれば、そのためには重労働になります。

In your case it ended up being a little light exercise, up and down the mountain.

あなた達の場合、山を登って下りただけの軽い運動で終わりました。

Good for your body *and* soul!"

体と精神には良かったでしょう！"

I looked at him sullenly, but what could we say?

私はふてくされた様子で彼を見ましたが、私たちは何を言えたでしょうか？

Had *we* done anything wrong?

私たちは何か間違いを犯したのでしょうか？

In the end he was right.

結局彼は正しかったのです。

We never made a cent off those damn rocks.

私たちは、あのいまいましい岩から１セントも得られることはありませんでした。

Though our dreams of vast wealth were dashed in that instant, we still fell in love with this beautiful area and we'll be back to visit again.

私たちの大きな富を得るという夢はその瞬間打ち砕かれましたが、あの美しい場所は素晴らしく、再び訪れることでしょう。

That is, if we ever have enough money for it.

つまり、そのための十分なお金があればということです。

44. The Ghost Cruise Liner

幽霊クルーズ船

It had always been a dream of ours to explore the Pacific.

私たちは、常に太平洋を探検することを夢見ていました。

It seemed the crown jewel of the world.

それは世界の至宝のようでした。

Just think, the numerous islands that dot that wild expanse, all rife with untold mystery.

考えてみてください。無数の島が一帯に散在しており、そこは語られざる謎で満ちています。

That's right, even my wife and son shared in this romance; I didn't have to do much convincing to get them to go on this trip.

そう、私の妻と息子にでさえこのロマンスを語っていたので、この旅行へ一緒に行くのに彼らを説得する必要はあまりありませんでした。

We meant to visit many of the islands in the western Pacific, but we decided to start our journey with a few leisurely days spent in Hawaii.

私たちは西太平洋にあるたくさんの島を訪れるつもりでしたが、この旅行の最初の数日間をハワイでのんびりと過ごすことにしました。

Though conventional and mired in all that is wrong with modern tourism, everything went swell for us there.

保守的で現代の観光の問題を見がちですが、全てがうまくいっていました。

Yes, everything was fine until we boarded that private jet headed for Saipan.

そう、サイパン行きのプライベートジェットに乗るまでは、全て順調だったのです。

Though I could not point to anything outwardly wrong with the scenario, as I buckled my seatbelt I whispered to my wife that I did not like the look of the Guamanian pilot.

一見このシナリオには何の間違いはなかったのですが、私はシートベルトを閉めて妻にあのグアム人パイロットの外見は好きじゃないとささやきました。

I had caught a glimpse of him before he disappeared into the cockpit: aside from his strange, shuffling gait, his uniform befitted the era of silent movies.

私は、彼が操舵席へ入っていくのをちらっと見ました。彼の奇妙な足を引きずる歩き方は別にして、彼の制服はサイレント映画の時代にふさわしいものでした。

A strange character indeed.

本当に変な人でした。

One hour into the flight the pilot noticed a strange cloud directly below us.

飛行してから1時間後、パイロットは私たちのすぐ下にある奇妙な雲に気づきました。

He informed us over the intercom that he believed something of gargantuan proportions must be situated under it.

彼は、インターコムを介して、私たちに下に何か大きなものがあるようだと伝えました。

My family and I became incredibly curious.

私の家族と私はそれにすごく興味を持ちました。

I opened the door to the cockpit and begged the captain to take us to a lower altitude so that we could better see what the phenomenon was.

私は操舵席のドアを開け、機長にそれが何なのかを見たいので、高度を下げてくれるようお願いしました。

As the plane descended, we slowly made out more and more detail.

飛行機が下降すると、少しずつその詳細が見えてきました。

Finally, we were able to make out what the large blotch upon the ocean actually was and were immediately struck dumb: a massive cruise ship that appeared ripped from another century entire, scorched black and partially destroyed, but still floating, as if animated by powers otherworldly.

ついに、海上にあるその大きなしみが見え呆然としました。別の世紀から現れ黒焦げて部分的に壊れている大きな旅客船でしたが浮いており、まるで別世界でした。

The water around the ship virtually glowed with a strange luminescence, a milky white shot through with tones of green.

その船の周囲にある水は実質的に奇妙な輝きを放っており、乳白色が緑の色調を突き抜けていました。

The pilot took the plane on several slow circuits around the wreckage so that we could soak up this unusual sight.

私たちがその不思議な光景をしばらく見られるように、パイロットは飛行機をその難破船の周りで何回かゆっくりと周回させました。

On closer inspection, we saw motion on the vessel's deck.

よく観察してみると、船の甲板で何かが動いているのを見ました。

Something or someone was moving about in rapid, jerking movements.

何かもしくは誰かが、素早くかつけいれん的に動き回っていました。

From above they looked like small ants scrambling across the deck's surface.

上空から見ると、彼らは甲板の上を動き回る小さなアリのように見えました。

But the harder we strained to make them out, the blurrier they became, if you can imagine that.

しかし、想像できると良いのですが、私たちが彼らを認識しようと努めるのが難しくなるにつれて、彼らの姿がはっきりしなくなりました。

In my mind's eye I imagined they were people, desperate for our help; they looked up at the sky in wonder at our appearance, and with clasped hands beseeched our pity.

私は心の中で、彼らは助けを求めている人々と想像しました。見上げた空で私達の姿を見て感嘆し、固く握られた手で私たちの哀れみを懇願するのでした。

My husband began to do some research on his laptop while the pilot circled the wreckage.

パイロットが難破船の周りを周回していた際、私の夫はノート型パソコンで何かを調べ始めました。

He googled the history of shipwrecks in this area of the globe, comparing the wreckage below to the images on the screen.

彼は、下にある難破船とスクリーンでの画像を比較しながら、グーグルでこの辺りにおける難破船の履歴について調べました。

"Pilot, take us a bit lower so that I can make out that wrecked ship better.

"パイロットさん、その難破船をもっとよく見えるようにもうちょっと下がってもらえませんか？

I can't quite discern enough details for a real comparison," my husband called in to the cockpit.

ちゃんと比較するのにはもうちょっと詳しく見る必要があります。"と夫は操舵席へ向かって言いました。

The pilot skillfully lowered our altitude until we were only about 100 yards or so above the wreckage.

パイロットは、難破船の上部から約100ヤード離れたところまで上手に高度を下げました。

We started to make out the details of the ship more clearly, but still, the little "ants" that raced about its deck remained a blur, like motes tickling the edge of one's vision.

私たちはよく見てみようとしましたが、甲板を走り回る小さな"アリ"は、まるでほこりが視界の端をくすぐるように、まだぼやけたままでした。

As we drew closer, everyone realized there was something *off* about this ship.

近づいていくと、皆はこの船は何かおかしいということに気づきました。

It looked like the Titanic, or else some ship out of a 19th century storybook, tricked out with antique steam stacks, rigging, and the like.

タイタニック号のような、もしくは19世紀の歴史本から出てきた船のようで、またそれは蒸気を出す古い煙突や索具などで飾り立てられていました。

My husband suddenly gasped.

私の夫は突然ハッと息をのみました。

"It cannot be," he said, "all things considered that wrecked ship there is the Kichi Maro!

"そんなはずはない。"と彼は言い、"総合的に考えるとあの難破船はきちまろです！

Or else it is the museum replica!

さもなければそれは博物館のレプリカです！

Look at this picture."

この写真を見てください。"

I simply couldn't believe it.

私はとにかく信じられませんでした。

It *was* the Kichi Maro, the Japanese cruise liner that sank during a typhoon on the 22nd of September 1912.

きちまろは、1922年9月22日の台風で沈んだ日本の大型客船でした。

It was a disaster that had claimed more than 1,000 lives, though it had been overshadowed by the tragic events of the Titanic.

タイタニック号の悲劇的な事件のために目立たなかったのですが、それは1000人以上の命を奪った大惨事でした。

Our immediate concern, aside from the delirious wonder we felt at finding a ship afloat that should have been resting at the bottom of the sea for at least a century, was the strange creatures crawling across the ship's deck.

少なくとも1世紀の間、海の底にあるはずの船が浮いているのを見て無我夢中になっていることとは別に、甲板をはっている奇妙な生き物が気になりました。

"They could be seals," I said to my husband.

"あれはアザラシです。"と私は夫に言いました。

"Honey, have you ever seen seals move like that?

"あのように動くアザラシを見たことありますか？

They flit hither and tither like a pack of spirits.

まるで魂のかたまりのようにあちらこちらに飛び回っています。

It is uncanny!"

あれは不気味です！"

"Pilot, can you get us any closer without risking our safety?

"パイロットさん、安全を確保しながらもう少し近づけますか？

No, ok…I think I can make out one of those things.

いや、大丈夫...たぶんそれらのうちの１つが見えると思います。

"It has two arms … no, I can't really say…"

それには２つの腕があり...いや、何とも言えません..."

"Let's take some pictures.

"何枚か写真を撮りましょう。

We can get them developed and later magnified.

現像した後に拡大してみましょう。

Then we may be able to make them out better," I said.

そうすれば、それらが何なのかよくわかると思います。"と私は言いました。

"This is the discovery of the century!

"これは世紀の発見です！

"Just think, the Kichi Maro, surfaced and nearly whole!"

考えてみてください。きちまろのほとんど全体が水面に浮上していたのです！"

A couple hours later we landed in Saipan without more ado.

これ以上の騒ぎはなく、2時間後私たちはサイパンに着陸しました。

We had the pictures developed at the local supermarket and we eagerly poured over them once back at our motel.

私たちは、現地のスーパーマーケットでその写真を現像し、モーテルに戻ると早速それを見てみました。

But lo and behold, they were all blank.

しかし、驚いたことにそれらはすべて真っ白でした。

Not only did they show nothing of the ship or the strange denizens we were so curious about, but they were utterly white.

そこには船もしくあの興味深い奇妙な住人は写っておらず、完全な白でした。

Like we had taken photographs of a blank, featureless wall.

まるで、何の特徴もない白い壁の写真を撮ったかのようでした。

Six months later we held a gathering of select friends in order to tell them of our strange discovery.

6ケ月後、その奇妙な発見を伝えるために、私たちは特定の友人たちを呼びました。

We related the circumstances surrounding the infamous Japanese cruise liner and showed them the photographs that had all come back mute and white.

私たちは、無名の日本の旅客船において起きた出来事を説明し、彼らにあの無言でかつ真っ白な写真を見せました。

They immediately heard the truth in our words and wanted to investigate this scene for themselves.

彼らは直接私たちの口から真実を聞くと、その現場を自分たちで調査してみたいと言いました。

We agreed to travel to the location by boat in order to get a closer look at the wreckage.

私たちは、その難破船についてもっとよく調べるために、船でその場所へ行くことに同意しました。

We rented a large sailing yacht in Guam and made directly for the spot, as my husband had saved the coordinates from the previous occasion.

私の夫は例の場所の座標を保存していたため、私たちはグアムで大きい帆走ヨットを借り、その場所へ向かいました。

We were nearly there when a violent storm suddenly overcame us; it felt and looked like a typhoon!

もう少しでたどり着くというところで、激しい嵐が私たちに向かってきました。どうやら台風のようです！

The yacht was equipped with all the modern radio and transmission devices you'd expect, but we were still caught completely unaware.

ヨットにはラジオと送信装置が備わっていましたが、私たちは完全に不意を突かれました。

It had not even appeared as a blip on the satellite image.

衛生画像上のピッという音としてさえ現れませんでした。

It seemed to have developed out of thin air, which was virtually impossible.

薄い空気から発達したように見えました。つまり実質的に不可能だったのです。

Just when we thought all was lost, with the waves lashing us about and the wind reaching a horrific crescendo, we entered a place of strange calm, like an oasis in the wild, belligerent waters.

波が私たちを激しく打ち付けかつ風が最高潮に達しもうダメだと思った時、妙に静かな場所へと入りました。そこは激しい海にあるオアシスのようでした。

We had evidently crossed into the eye of the typhoon, and what do you know, there she was: the magnificent, decadent Kichi Maro.

私たちはどうやら台風の目の中へ入り、何と、そこには壮大で退廃的なきちまろがいたのです。

" I told you!" I shouted to our friends.

"言ったでしょ！"と私は友人たちに向かって叫びました。

They all looked at the gigantic wreck in dismay.

彼らは、がっかりしてその巨大な難破船を見ていました。

It loomed over us, in all its broken glory.

それは、壊れた荘厳さを保ちながらも私たちの前にぼんやりと現れました。

We drew closer and discovered that the ship was covered in vast scars, black swaths that looked like the result of fire.

私たちは近づいてみると、その船には火事の跡のような大きな傷で覆われていることがわかりました。

Large parts of the ship were covered in broken coral, a sickly brand of grey invertebrate that wrapped itself around the ship like a monstrous python.

船の大部分は壊れたサンゴで覆われていました。それは、巨大なニシキヘビのように自ら船を巻きつけている活気のない灰色の無脊椎動物でした。

All the chimneys were missing; the blown-out windows gaped at us ominously.

全ての煙突は無くなっていました。また、吹き飛ばされた窓が、私たちを不気味に眺めていました。

We saw the creatures moving again as we got closer to the ship, but try as we did, we could make out nothing more than blurs.

船に近づくと、またあの生き物が動き回っているのが見えましたが、やはりぼやけているものしか見えませんでした。

A few us snapped photographs.

何枚か写真を撮りました。

When we were only a hand's width away, I reached out and touched the great grey hull.

手の届くところまで来たら、私は手を伸ばして巨大な灰色の船体に触りました。

It was pulsing and vaguely warm.

それは脈を打っており何となく暖かかったです。

I looked up and noticed dark clouds closing in and urged my husband to steer us away.

私は見上げると黒い雲が近づいてきているのが見え、夫にそれから遠ざかるよう促しました。

The storm began to rage around us again, and the water became nearly as choppy as before.

嵐は私たちの周囲で再び激しくなり、海も以前と同じように荒くなってきました。

But strangely enough, directly in front of our yacht, the way was clear and placid.

しかし、奇妙なことに私たちのヨットのちょうど前方の道は晴れておりかつ静かでした。

It was like a strange force guided us through the storm, making way for the yacht.

嵐の中、不思議な力が私たちを導いて、ヨットための道を作ってくれたようでした。

Soon we were back upon untroubled waters.

すぐに私たちは静かな海へと戻りました。

We never talked much about that experience.

私たちは、この体験についてあまり語ることはありませんでした。

None of us did.

誰もがです。

It had chilled us to the bone and forced a pact of silence upon us.

それは私たちを骨まで冷たくさせ、そして黙らせました。

The crew split up after we anchored, all going their separate ways, back to a world that thereafter made less sense.

いかりを下ろした後、私たちは別々の道を通ってこれまで以上に無意味となった世界へと帰っていきました。

The pictures I developed were again, as you can probably already guess, entirely blank.

恐らくすでにおわかりだと思うのですが、私が現像した写真はやはり真っ白でした。

45. A World of Silence

静かな世界

I am a so-called movie producer.

私はいわゆる映画プロデューサーです。

I say "so-called" because I have never actually had any success in the industry; alas, I am trying to keep the dream alive.

"いわゆる"と言ったのは、私はこの業界で成功したことがないからです。悲しいかな、まだ夢を追い続けているのです。

Having had several failed stints in the United States, I thought to try my luck in Japan.

アメリカでの失敗を何回か繰り返し、次に私は日本で運を試そうと思いました。

My love of b-movies and monster films might just give me an edge in the Land of the Rising Sun.

私のB級映画と怪物映画への愛は、私を日出づる国で成功させてくれるかもしれません。

I was buzzing through Tokyo on an express-train, one of those modern contraptions which glide along the rails in virtual silence.

私は、実質的に静かにレールを滑る現代のからくりの１つである急行列車を使って、東京を歩き回りました。

I looked out the window at Tokyo, this most fabulous of cities, taking in all the colors and marvels that seem particular to this city and people.

私は窓越しでとても素晴らしい都市である東京を眺めました。そこには、この都市とそこの人々に独特であろう全ての色と驚きで散りばめられていました。

The skyscrapers marched to the edge of my vision, thrusting up into the clouds like a future metropolis from some pulp novel.

超高層ビルは私の視界の端まで行進し、大衆小説に出てくる未来の大都市のように雲を突き上げていました。

Ruminating so, I was suddenly inspired: what if Tokyo could serve as a metaphor for silence?

そのように思いを巡らしていたら、急にひらめきました。もし東京を静寂の隠喩として使えるとしたらどうでしょうか？

A movie about…silence.

静寂...に関する映画。

And Tokyo as its backdrop, its protagonist.

そして、その背景と主役としての東京。

Later, walking the streets of the city, the silence was what struck me.

その後、道を歩いていたら静寂が私を襲いました。

Here I was, standing in the heart of one of earth's most bustling cities, and I was enveloped in silence.

私は、地球で最も活気のある都市の１つの中心地に立ち、静寂に包まれました。

Sure, there were noises galore.

当然、そこではたくさんの雑音が聞こえます。

Of course, there were cars and buses; the clinking sounds of arcades reached one on every street.

もちろん、そこには車やバスがあり、すべての通りでアーケードのチャリンと鳴る音が1つに聞こえました。

But still, I felt encased in a bubble.

しかし、まだ私はバブルに包み込まれているように感じました。

It was like I was looking at the world through glass; I could hear the sounds, but they never really *reached* me.

ガラス越しで世界を見ているようでした。そこではたくさんの音が聞こえますが、それらは私に実際には届かないのです。

It was at this point that I started to doubt my sanity.

この時、私は自分の正気を疑い始めました。

I tried and tried, but even here the movie industry rejected me.

何度も試しましたが、ここでさえも映画業界は私を拒絶しました。

I sent them tapes.

私は彼らに映画の録画テープを送りました。

I did audition after audition.

何度もオーディションを受けました。

I even tried my hand at writing scripts, but none of it bore fruit.

試しに自分で脚本を書いてみましたが、何の成果も得られませんでした。

I had a stack of rejection letters to prove it.

私は、それを証明できるたくさんの不採用通知を持っていました。

Still I did not give up.

まだ私はあきらめていませんでした。

I kept harboring the dream of seeing my work on the silver screen.

私は、自分の映画が銀幕で観られる夢を抱き続けていました。

That's why when I heard a few Americans talking about movies at a local café, I scooted my chair closer and joined in the conversation.

だから私は、数名のアメリカ人が地元のカフエで映画について話しているのを聞いた時、自分の椅子を近くに引き寄せてその会話に加わったのです。

Turns out we were all of a like mind; they had also traveled to Japan in the hopes of making it in the film industry.

結局、私たちは同じことを考えていたのです。つまり、彼らも日本に来て映画業界で成功したいと思っていたのです。

They were a group of writers mostly.

彼らのほとんどはライターでした。

One woman even was an accomplished author.

ある1人の女性はベテランの作家でした。

"You know, I'm an accomplished director myself," I told them casually.

"あの、私はベテランの映画監督なのです。"と私は彼らに何気なく言いました。

I wanted to appear like I had no worries about making it in the industry myself.

私は、あたかも業界で何の心配もなくうまくやっていけるかのように思われたかったのです。

The woman smiled.

その女性は微笑みました。

"Actually we have been looking for a bona fide director."

"実は、私たちは本物の映画監督を探しています。"

ventured a young guy, who had introduced himself as a lighting specialist.

と照明のスペシャリストとして自己紹介した若い男性が、思い切って言いました。

This was when I could still hear things, and I nodded my head as suavely as possible,

この時はまだ冷静に話を聞ける状態で、私はできるだけ丁寧にうなずきました。

We talked long into the afternoon that day, and we all left full of hope and ideas, agreeing to meet back in two days' time to consolidate our efforts and make a real sci-fi flick, something we would all be proud of.

私たちはその日の午後中ずっと話をし、たくさんの希望やアイディアで溢れ、それらをまとめて本当のSF映画にするために二日後にまた会うことになりました。

We decided to make it a very short film, a pilot of sorts that would be a tease just to get the studios curious about our work.

私たちは、非常に短い映画を作ることにしました。映画会社が私たちの仕事に興味を持ってもらうためのじらし広告である、ちょっとしたパイロットです。

We worked so well as a team that we finished shooting in a matter of days.

私たちはチームとして非常によく働いたため、撮影は数日中に終わりました。

I was full of inspiration and insisted that the film be completely silent.

私はひらめきで満たされており、映画は完全に無声にするべきだと主張しました。

I wanted to let my cinematography do most of the work; I really wanted to capture the oppressive *silence* of the city about me.

私は、自身の映画撮影技術を使って、あの街の耐えがたいほどの静寂を捉えたかったのです。

As a matter of fact, Tokyo was the driving force behind all that occurred in our short sci-fi piece.

実を言うと、私たちの短編SF映画で起こった全ての原動力は、東京でした。

It generated the entire mood; I simply could not have done it in any other city.

それは全体のムードを作ってくれました。他のどの都市でもそれを行うことはできなかったでしょう。

The weeks after we completed filming were some of the best of my life.

撮影が終わってから数週間は、私の人生で最高の気分でした。

I knew that the industry was now open before me, and that my break would be coming any day now.

映画業界は今や私を待ち受けており、私の好機はいつ訪れてもおかしくなかったでしょう。

I walked around the city in a blissful state, absorbing everything Tokyo had to offer: the botanical gardens, the strange cuisine, the arcades, and not least, the movie halls, where they showed films that I could barely fathom.

私は至福の気分で街を歩き回り、東京の全てを吸収しました。植物園、奇妙な料理、アーケード、特に私がほとんど理解できない映画を上映している映画館。

But towards the end of the second week, I started to notice something very odd: I heard less and less.

しかし、2週目の週末にかけて、私は何かとても変なことに気づいたのです。次第に聞こえなくなったのです。

The stimuli of the city became more and more visual, and sounds began to recede.

この街の刺激はますます視覚化される一方で、音が無くなり始めたのです。

Soon my walk through the botanical garden was not accompanied by bird song and running water.

植物園の中を歩いていると、鳥の歌声や流れる水の音が聞こえてきませんでした。

The arcades were full of neon light, but I no longer heard the beeping machines.

アーケードにはたくさんのネオンの光がありましたが、もはや機械音は聞こえませんでした。

And it was the same in the theatres: every movie was now silent.

映画館でも同様で、全ての映画は無声です。

The scariest episode during this time was when I met my "colleagues", those who had helped me make the sci-fi film, at the selfsame café.

この間、最も恐ろしいと感じたのは、あのSF映画の制作を手伝ってくれた"仲間たち"と例のカフェで会った時でした。

I pulled up my chair and they just stared at me as if they had never seen me before.

私は自分のイスを引っ張って行って、彼らはまるで初めて会ったかのように私をじっと見ていました。

With looks of perplexity on their faces, they tried to find out what I wanted.

彼らの困惑した顔から察するに、彼らは私が何を求めているのか探ろうとしていました。

Or, at least I think they did.

もしくは、少なくとも彼らはそうしたのでしょう。

See, I could not *hear* them.

ほら、私は彼らが何を言っているのか聞こえませんでした。

I just stared at their moving lips, a kind of disquiet now bubbling in the pit of my stomach.

私は、彼らの唇の動きをじっと見つめました。この時、一種の不安が私の胃にある穴で泡立っていました。

I rushed from the café like a madman bent on escaping an institution.

私は、施設から逃げようと夢中になっている狂人のように急いでカフェを出ました。

I scheduled an appointment with a doctor, for I was now sure that I had done irreversible damage to my hearing.

私は、自分の聴覚に取り返しのつかない損傷を与えてしまったことを確信したため、医者の予約を取りました。

I could not even hear my own voice.

自分の声さえ聞こえませんでした。

When he saw me, I tried to explain my condition, but speech failed me; as it is with the born deaf, without hearing my own voice I simply became a stuttering, inarticulate mess.

彼が私と会った時、私は自分の症状を説明しようとしてもできませんでした。生まれつきの難聴のようで、自分の声を聞かずに吃音になり、不明瞭な混乱でした。

I was forced to write everything down, and he did the same for me.

私は、筆記するよう言われ、彼も同様のことをしました。

He told me that he had a special injection that he would give me, something that might stimulate my faculties of hearing.

彼は私に、私の聴覚能力を刺激するかもしれない特別な注射を私に打つと言いました。

The last thing I remember is staring up at the ceiling while he prepared the syringe, hoping that this would cure me.

最後に覚えているのは、彼が注射を準備している間、それが私を治してくれるのを願いながら天井を見つめていたことです。

I woke up sometime later in a hospital.

しばらくしてから、私は病院で目を覚ましました。

I knew immediately it was not the doctor's office.

すぐに、ここはあの医者の部屋ではないと気づきました。

It was vast and filled with a number of patients, some with their heads bandaged, some walking the aisles on crutches, tongues lolling like dogs, their eyes mad and searching.

そこは広くてたくさんの患者がいました。頭に包帯を巻いている人、松葉杖を使って廊下を歩いている人、犬のように舌がたれており、狂った目で何かを探していました。

What was this place?

この場所は何なのでしょうか？

I drifted off to sleep again, as the injection still had me drowsy and drugged.

あの注射のためにまだ眠たくてもうろうとしていたため、私は再び眠りにつきました。

Something shook me awake in a rude fashion.

何かが無理矢理私の目を覚まさせました。

I stared up into the face of a nurse who scribbled something on a note and held it up to me: *this is a place of silence.*

私は、ノートに何かを走り書きしてそれを私に掲げた看護師の顔を見上げました。ここは静かな場所です。

Under no circumstances are noises allowed or you will be punished.

いかなる状況でも騒いではいけません。さもなければ罰せられます。

To this day I am still here, in the ward of absolute silence.

今日に至るまで、私はまだここにいます。完全に静かな病室です。

I've been abused several times.

私は数回虐待されました。

I look out on Tokyo's skyline, which is quite visible from my personal cell's lone window, and wonder at what all the denizens are hearing in a city so teeming with life.

私は、自分の独房にある唯一の窓からよく見える東京のスカイラインを見上げ、人生で溢れかえっているそこの住人は一体何を聞いているのだろうと思いました。

I hope this note and all that I have written finds someone.

この覚書と私が書いたもの全てが、誰かに見つかることを願っています。

It is my only way out.

それが唯一の私の脱出方法です。

Can anyone hear me?

誰か私が聞こえますか？

46. The Cherry Blossom Stones

桜の石

My husband and I have always been adventure-minded people.

私の夫と私は常に冒険心を持っています。

In fact, that's really the reason we first decided to start dating.

事実、私たちはそれが理由で付き合い始めました。

I still remember our first encounter, when I said my real passion was to *explore*.

私は、最初に出会った時に私が本当に好きなことは探検だと言ったことを、まだ覚えています。

Now, when I say "explore", I don't mean the forays reserved for the bourgeoisie, but the good, honest, off-the-beaten-track kind.

さて、私が言っている"探検"とは、ブルジョアジーのために予約された旅行のことではなく、素晴らしくて素朴な、一種の普通ではないものを指します。

That's why when we began to plan our honeymoon together, we considered long and hard which mysterious country we'd like to visit most.

だから私たちが新婚旅行の計画を立て始めた時、どの神秘的な国へ一番行きたいか長い時間をかけてたくさん考えました。

We ended up settling on Japan, given the airy mists which seem to hang about that land in one's imagination, and we were not disappointed in our choice.

その土地に付きまとっているような軽快な霧を想像して、結局日本へ行くことにしました。そして、私たちはその選択についてがっかりすることはありませんでした。

You will soon see why.

その理由は後でわかることでしょう。

We thought the best way to really see and explore Japan was by cruise ship.

私たちは、日本をちゃんと見て回るにはクルーズ船が一番いいと思いました。

Plus, we would have all the added benefits that a cruise liner has to provide: the unlimited food and alcohol, heated pools, and social activities.

加えて、クルーズ船では無制限の食べ物やお酒、温水プール、グループ活動を楽しめます。

It really was like killing two birds with one stone.

本当に一石二鳥でした。

Japan also held a special allure for my husband, for he is an avid collector of precious stones.

私の夫は非常に熱心に貴重な石を集めているため、彼にとって日本は魅力的でした。

Since he was a little boy, he has hoarded stones bought and found, from the simple purple quartz to the more exclusive forms of fossils which formed the cream of the crop of his collection.

彼は少年の頃から、単純な紫色の石英から彼の最も貴重なコレクションである唯一の化石まで様々な石を買ったり探したりしていました。

There was one stone in particular that my husband had always sought, and that was the "cherry blossom stone", native to Japan.

夫がいつも特に探し求めていた１つの石がありました。それは、日本原産の"桜の石"でした。

It is said that they are typically found embedded in hornfels, whose metamorphic process aids in the cherry blossom's development.

それはよくホルンフェルスで見つかると言われていました。ホルンフェルスの変成プロセスが、桜の石の形成を助けます。

These stones are *often* found in the caves of Honshu Island, off the coast of southern Japan.

これらの石はよく本州にある洞穴で見つかります。日本の南方にある海岸沖です。

Now you start to see why my husband pined so much for a honeymoon cruising these straits.

これでなぜ私の夫が、新婚旅行にこれらの海峡を船で回ることを切望しているのかわかり始めたことでしょう。

Fortunately, our ship was scheduled to dock at Himeji port, and we knew that there were supposedly caves rich in cherry blossom stones thereabouts, as long as one was able to find a guide willing to take a foreigner into these sacred regions.

幸運なことに私たちの船は姫路港で停泊する予定で、その辺には桜の石がたくさんある洞穴がありますが、そこまで連れて行ってくれるガイドが必要でした。

With a little bit of persistence and pestering of the locals, we were given directions to a man who might be able to lead us to one of the caves.

地元の人々をほとんど悩ませる必要もなく、私たちは１つの洞穴へ連れて行ってくれるかもしれない、ある男性の居場所を教えてもらうことができました。

He lived in a little fishing shack on the edge of town, and when we approached his abode, we saw smoke rising from the chimney into the crisp morning air.

彼は、町の端にある小さな釣り小屋に住んでおり、私たちが彼の住居に近づいたら、煙が煙突から爽やかな朝の空気に向かって出ていました。

We knocked several times before a shrunken, crabby old man opened the front door, wearing a kasa and blinking at us sheepishly.

私たちは何回かドアをたたくと、背が低く気難しい老人男性が正面のドアを開けました。彼は笠を被っており、私たちに向かって気弱そうに瞬きをしていました。

"Good morning sir," said my husband, "we were told that you may guide us to the caves where the famous cherry blossom stones lie."

"おはようございます。"と夫が言いました。"私たちは、あなたが私たちを有名な桜の石がある洞穴へ連れて行ってくれるかもしれないと言われました。"

At first, I was sure that he did not speak nor understand English, as he just stared at my husband with a sour expression.

当初、彼は不機嫌な顔つきで夫を見つめていたため、私は彼が英語を話せないか理解できないことを確信していました。

But after several moments, he answered him in heavily accented English.

しかし、しばらくして彼は訛りの強い英語で彼に答えました。

"I do. But…"

"はい。しかし…"

"Yes? I'm a collector.

"はい？私は収集家です。

"I also have a lot of cash."

また、たくさんの現金もあります。"

My husband proceeded to flash him a fistful of Japanese yen.

夫はたくさんの日本円をちらっと見せ始めました。

"I understand," said the old man.

"わかりました。"とその老人男性は言いました。

It seemed decided.

決まったようでした。

Little else was spoken between us before setting off.

出発するまでに、私たちの間でそれほど話をしませんでした。

The cave mouth he led us to was yawning and dark, so dark that our eyes could not discern much past several yards.

彼が連れて行ってくれた洞穴の入り口は大きく暗かったです。暗過ぎたため、数ヤードを進むと目の前のものを識別できませんでした。

To get there the guide led us through a ravine and across a valley, through forest and over field alike, and we became disoriented.

そこへ行くのに、ガイドは私たちを連れて渓谷、谷、森、田畑を越え、私たちは混乱してしまいました。

We did not even know which direction the port of Himeji now lay.

姫路港がどちらの方角にあるのかさえ、わからなくなってしまいました。

If it were not for our sure-footed guide, we would have been quite beside ourselves, even though we likened ourselves "explorers".

私たちは自分たちを"探検家"になぞらえたとしても、確かなガイドがいなければ私たちは取り乱してしまったことでしょう。

That said, we were admittedly hesitant to enter the cave mouth.

とは言え、私たちは確かに洞穴の入り口へ入るのをためらいました。

It looked so foreboding.

とても不吉な予感がしました。

But our little guide reassured us with kind words.

しかし、私たちの小さなガイドは優しい言葉で私たちを安心させました。

"Don't worry."

"大丈夫です。

"Mr. Akira see you through."

アキラさん、見てください。

"I have an electric lantern."

私は電気ランタンを持っています。

With the help of Mr. Akira's lantern, we slowly made our way into the cave and started to explore its depths.

アキラさんのランタンの助けを借り、私たちは少しずつ洞穴の中を進み、その深いところを探索し始めました。

It seemed that it had no end, and as we got deeper into its warrens, we noticed that a thick moisture clung to the walls, slimy and faintly luminescent.

終わりがないようでした。その入り組んだ迷路へ入っていくと、厚くて湿っている何かが壁にくっついているのに気づき、それはぬるぬるして微かに発光していました。

We asked our guide about this, but he was strangely silent on the matter.

私たちはこれについてガイドに尋ねましたが、彼はそのことについて妙に黙っていました。

He brought up our rear, holding the lantern aloft while my husband chose which passage to take.

夫がどの道へ進むべきか選んでいた間、彼は私たちの後ろでランタンを高く持ち上げていました。

Suddenly my husband stopped and said that he thought we must turn around; this was evidently not the way to the hoard of stones.

突然、夫が立ち止まり、私たちは引き返さなければいけないと言いました。これは、明らかに石の宝庫へつながる道ではありませんでした。

It was then that the cave was thrown into utter darkness.

その時、洞穴の中は真っ暗闇となりました。

It was like all life had been snuffed out.

まるで、全ての生き物が根絶されたかのようでした。

We called out for Mr. Akira, but he did not respond.

私たちはアキラさんを呼びましたが、彼は返事をしませんでした。

"Where did he go?

"彼はどこへ行ったのでしょうか？

"Was this some kind of hoax?"

これは一種の作り話だったのでしょうか？"

My husband groped for me in the dark.

夫は暗闇の中を手探りで私を探しました。

"I have my cell phone.

"私は自分の携帯電話を持っています。

"I can use the flashlight app," I said reassuringly.

懐中電灯アプリを使えます。"と私は安心させるように言いました。

We could see now, though somewhat sparingly.

それほどではないですが、見えるようになりました。

The weak light of the phone only illuminated what was directly in front of us.

弱い携帯電話の照明は、私たちの目の前を照らすだけでした。

Nevertheless, there was no sign of our guide, Mr. Akira.

それでもなお、私たちのガイドであるアキラさんの形跡はありませんでした。

It was like he had suddenly vanished into thin air.

まるで、彼は突然薄い空気の中へ消えたかのようでした。

"What are we going to do now?

"どうしましょう？

We only have a little over 6 hours before we need to be back at the ship".

私たちは、あと6時間強で船に戻らなければなりません。"

"I don't know.

"わかりません。

Let's try to backtrack while we still have light from your phone.

あなたの携帯電話の照明をまだ使える間に、来た時と同じ道を引き返してみましょう。

We were terribly scared, verging on panic.

私たちはひどく怯えており、パニックになりそうでした。

I could hear my husband's ragged breathing in front of me.

私は、前方の荒々しい夫の息が聞こえました。

He seemed to be picking directions at random, becoming more and more desperate.

彼は手当たり次第に方向を決めていたようで、ますます必死になっていきました。

When all seemed lost, we entered a chamber that was bathed in golden light.

もうダメだと思った時、私たちは金色の光を浴びた部屋へ入っていきました。

There were stones and crystals everywhere, of all sizes and dimensions, specimens that were worth small fortunes.

そこには、至る所に様々な大きさの石やクリスタルがあり、それらは小さな幸運に値するものでした。

My husband said he couldn't believe it; he was quite lost for words.

夫は信じられないと言いました。彼は言葉を失っていました。

It was like coming to the end of the rainbow and discovering the mythic pot of gold.

まるで、虹の先端にたどりついて、金でできた神話上のつぼを発見したかのようでした。

Alas, I told my husband we couldn't linger; my phone's battery was almost dead.

残念ながら、私は携帯電話の電池がそろそろ切れるので長居はできないと、夫に言いました。

He had begun to fill his pockets, choosing stones he deemed most exemplary.

彼は、最も価値のあると思われる石を選んで、ポケットに入れ始めました。

I snapped a few photographs before my husband told me not to waste any more of the battery.

私が数枚の写真を撮ったら、夫はこれ以上電池を無駄に使うなと私に言いました。

"Please, honey, just fill your pockets with stones.

"お願いです。石を拾ってポケットの中に入れてください。

Don't worry about pictures.

写真について心配しなくて大丈夫です。

We are rich!"

私たちは金持ちですから！"

Now burdened by our load, we left the chamber on its opposite end, following the repeated sound of what we thought was a great gong being rung.

そして私たちはかなり重くなりました。その部屋を出てその反対側の方へ行き、

何度もゴーンと大きく鳴っている音が聞こえる方向へ向かいました。

This "gong" became clearer as we continued in this direction, and we eventually found a tunnel with daylight at the end.

この方向へ進み続けると同時に、"ゴーン"という音は明確になってきました。ついに、私たちは日光が先の方で見えるトンネルをみつけたのです。

We had made it.

何とかなりました。

When we got back to civilization, it was difficult to find a taxi to take us to the port, as nobody seemed to understand a lick of English.

文明社会にもどった時、そこでは誰も少しの英語もわからないため、私たちを港まで連れて行ってくれるタクシーを探すのは困難でした。

We finally convinced a shady looking fellow in an unmarked car to take us back to the ship, but he demanded an exuberant amount of money once we were parked at the dock.

ついに、標識のない車に乗っている、うさんくさい顔つきののドライバーに船のところまで行ってもらいましたが、到着後、彼は高額の料金を要求しました。

"I'm sorry…I have no more money.

"すみません…これ以上お金はないのです。

"But, .. I do have…these rocks."

しかし、..持っています…これらの石なら"

My husband prodded me to show him a few examples from my pockets.

夫は、私にいくらかのそれをポケットから出して、彼に見せるよう促しました。

The driver, who omitted an air of electric violence, snatched them out of my hand and scrutinized them.

ドライバーは暴力的な空気を退け、それらを夫からつかみとってから注意深く見ました。

"Give them to me."

それらを私(わたくし)にください。

"All of them."

全部(ぜんぶ)です。

"Or I kill you."

さもなければあなたたちを殺(ころ)します。

Needless to say, we gave him most of our findings.

言(い)うまでもなく、私(わたくし)たちは発見(はっけん)したほとんどのものを彼(かれ)にあげました。

We hightailed it out of there and onto our ship before he could demand more.

彼(かれ)がさらに要求(ようきゅう)する前(まえ)に、私(わたくし)たちは急(いそ)いでそこから去(さ)り私(わたくし)たちの船(ふね)の方(ほう)へ向(む)かいました。

At least my husband got to keep a few of his favorite samples.

少(すく)なくとも、夫(おっと)は彼(かれ)の好(す)きな数個(すうこ)の石(いし)をまだ持(も)っていました。

Though we didn't have much to show for when we eventually arrived back home, the few photos I took attested to our marvelous discovery.

私たちが家に帰った時、見せられるものはそれほどありませんでしたが、私が撮った数枚の写真が私たちの驚くべき発見を裏付けました。

On social media it became known as "The Cave of Delights", and we are now known as that *daring* couple, explorers of the first order.

ソーシャルメディアでは、それは"喜びの洞穴"として有名になり、今では私たちは大胆なカップルで一流の探検家として知られています。

We may not have gotten rich, but at least we are famous.

私たちはお金持ちにならなかったかもしれませんが、少なくとも有名になりました。

47. Humor is if you still laugh

ユーモアは笑っているときに

I wanted to go to Japan for a long time. I never met a real Japanese person in my country.

私は長い間、日本に行きたいと思っていました。私がいる国では、今まで日本人に会ったことがありません。

When I finally arrived for the first time in Japan, I noticed all these serious faces.

とうとう、初めて日本に到着したとき、私はたくさんの人々が真剣な顔をしていることに気がつきました。

Even in the trains, there was not much speaking.

電車の中であっても、誰も話をしていません。

Sometimes, I nodded at strangers. I wanted to talk to them, make some friends on the trip like I did in so many other countries.

ときどき、日本人にお辞儀をしました。他の国での旅行で友達をつくったときのように、私は話しかけたかったのです。

In Italy and in Brazil, starting a conversation with strangers was never an issue.

イタリアやブラジルでは、初めて会う人々と会話をするのに、何も問題はありませんでした。

I decided I needed to break the ice, to get some life into their heads, so to speak. How about some humor from a real human being, not from a TV comedy? So, one morning, I stepped into the subway train.

なので、私はこの氷をとかし、会話をする決心をしました。テレビのコメディ番組ではなく、目の前にいる人間によるユーモアはおもしろいかもしれない？と考え、ある朝、地下鉄に乗りました。

I saw all these serious faces, nobody seemed to be alive.

いたるところにある真剣な顔、誰も生きている気配がありません。

I took a deep breath, and shouted: "Hi, I am Japanese, I am Japanese!"

大きく息をすいこみ、「こんにちは、私は日本人です、日本人です！」とさけびました。

But nobody was laughing. I shouted a little louder so they would understand the humor.

しかし、だれも笑わなかったので、ユーモアをわかってもらえるよう、

私は少し声を大きくしてさけびました。

A man said something I couldn't understand, but it wasn't a friendly remark, that I could tell.

ある男性が、はっきりとはわからなかったのですが、あまり親しくない様子で何かを

言いました。

Suddenly, a woman accused me in English of being a liar. I told her this was a joke. She didn't believe me, and repeated I was a liar.

すると突然、女性が英語で私が嘘をついていると言いました。私が彼女にこれは冗談であると説明しましたが、彼女は信じず、嘘つきだと言い続けました。

The next morning, I flew to Brazil.

そして翌朝、私はブラジルに帰りました。

48. The treasure in the forest
No Furigana, old character style

森の中の宝物

John Smith is a romantic person.
ジョン・スミスは、ロマンチックな人です。

Although he was already 18 years old at that time, he was more interested in history books than in young ladies, other than his friends and classmates.
彼は当時１８歳でしたが、若い女性や友達、クラスメートよりも歴史の本にずっと興味がありました。

When he didn't sleep or he wasn't busy with his homework he used to doze on the sofa and was dreaming of having lots of money one day.
彼は眠らないとき、または宿題で忙しい時、ソファの上でうたた寝をして、いつかたくさんのお金を稼ぐ夢を見ることをよくしていました。

One afternoon he fell asleep on the couch.
ある午後、彼はカウチで眠りに落ちました。

He had a lively dream.
彼は生き生きとした夢を見ました。

He dreamed to have found a treasure in the woods.
彼は森の中で宝物を見つける夢を見ました。

As he found a chest, he opened it and a little cloud of smoke came out, and an old voice said:
彼は宝箱を見つけて、彼がそれを開けると、煙の小さな塊が出てきて、老人の声がしました。

Go to the forest, you will find a map there.
「森へ行きなさい。そこに地図があるでしょう。

The map will be buried beneath an old pine tree.
地図は古い松の木の真下に埋められています。

Dig a hole where you'll see some smoke fuming.
煙が出ているところに穴を掘りなさい。

It's a treasure map.
それが宝の地図です。

You can become rich if you find the map.
その地図を見つければ、あなたはお金持ちになるでしょう。」

The smoke came closer to his face,
煙が彼の顔に近づいてきました。

John couldn't breathe anymore, and he thought to be choking.
彼はもはや息ができず、窒息するかと思いました。

He woke up in the afternoon.
彼は午後に目を覚ましました。

He knew there must have been a treasure in the forest!
彼には、森に宝があることがわかっていました！

Behind the house a path began, which lead directly to the forest.
家の裏から始まる小道があり、森へまっすぐ続いています。

He followed the track and saw the pine tree.
彼は跡をたどり、松の木を見つけました。

This was the place!
ここがその場所だ！

John dug into the soil and found a little tube and inside he found a rolled-up scroll.
ジョンは土の中を掘って、小さなチューブを見つけ、中には丸まった巻物が入っていました。

It looked like a Buddhist scroll.
それは仏教の巻物のようでした。

He rolled it up and went home.
彼は丸めて家に帰りました。

The next day he went to a pawn-shop.
次の日、彼は質屋に行きました。

He didn't get any money for the map.
彼は地図でお金をもらえませんでした。

John went home and fell asleep.

彼は家に帰って眠りました。

He dreamed that he would never need any more money.
彼はもうお金が必要でなくなった夢を見ました。

As he woke up he glanced smiling at the treasure map.
彼は目を覚ますと、地図を微笑んで見ました。

The money and the treasure were not important to him anymore.

お金と地図は彼にとってもう重要ではありませんでした。

49. A Special Cooking Course

特別(とくべつ)なクッキングコース

My wife and I spent last year on one of the new cruise lines around the southern half of Japan.

去年(きょねん)、私(わたくし)の妻(つま)と私(わたくし)は、日本(にほん)の南側(みなみがわ)を巡(めぐ)る新(あたら)しいクルーズ船(ふね)の1つで過(す)ごしました。

It was upon the Merry Princess, a 2,500-passenger behemoth that contained every luxury and distraction that a modern man could possibly crave.

それは、現代(げんだい)の男性(だんせい)が羨(うらや)むであろう贅沢(ぜいたく)と娯楽(ごらく)を有(ゆう)し、2500人(にん)の乗客(じょうきゃく)を抱(かか)える巨大(きょだい)なクルーズ船(せん)である、メリープリンセスでした。

We both found it to be a relaxing, easy and relatively inexpensive way to explore some of the more "off-the-beaten-path" areas of the country.

私(わたくし)たちは、この船旅(ふなたび)は落(お)ち着(つ)いてかつゆったりしていると思(おも)いました。そして、その国(くに)の"普通(ふつう)ではない"場所(ばしょ)を見(み)る方法(ほうほう)としては比較的安(ひかくてきやす)いでしょう。

We were having a grand time, and we both experienced the peace of mind that comes from untethering yourself from the troubles of daily life.

私たちはすてきな時間を過ごし、日々のトラブルから解放することにより心が休まりました。

That is why I was so shocked to one day wake up and find myself in a hospital bed.

だからこそ、私はある日目が覚めて、病院のベッドの上にいることに気づいた時とてもショックでした。

It was certainly not the way I had envisioned ending our cruise.

私たちのクルーズ船の旅は、このような結末になるはずではありませんでした。

We stopped in Beppu, a spa town designed for tourists and built over an active geothermal area.

私たちは別府に停留しました。別府は旅行客のために計画された温泉街であり、活発な地熱地帯で構築されました。

This feature afforded the town nine small clusters of hot springs and geysers known, somewhat cheekily, as "The Hells".

この温泉街の特徴は温泉と間欠泉で構成される9つの小さな集団で、やや大げさですが"地獄"として知られています。

English was not widely spoken here and the signs about the town were just an indiscernible jumble of Japanese kanji.

そこでは、あまり英語が通じず、町の標識にはゴチャゴチャしていて見分けにくい日本語の漢字が書かれていました。

To find oneself without bearings, that is the mark of true adventure, or at least that is what I tried to tell myself at the time.

自分自身で迷うことは真の探検の象徴、もしくはそれは少なくとも当時私が自分自身に伝えようとしたことでした。

We dipped our toes into the culture without putting our *entire* foot in, and I think we were all the happier for it.

私たちは、足全体ではなくつま先だけをその文化に浸すだけで満足していました。

My wife already knew a little about the local culture, so she helped me when I was most ill at ease.

私の妻は、日本文化について少しだけ知っていたので、私がすごく不安に思った時に助けてくれました。

One of the activities we chose was a cooking course conducted in one of the many beautiful parks around Beppu.

たくさんあるアクティビティーの中から、私たちは別府市の近くにある美しい公園の1つで行われたクッキングコースを選びました。

I already knew a thing or two about Japanese cooking and cuisine, but I was far from being a pro.

私は、日本料理について1つあるいは2つのことを知っていましたが、プロとは程遠かったです。

I've never been a fan of sushi nor shabu-shabu, and I generally prefer my Asian food to be of the shopping mall variety.

私は、寿司もしくはシャブシャブが好きではなく、普段はショッピングモールにある様々なアジア料理を好みます。

But I wanted to humor my wife so I agreed to take part in the course.

しかし、私は妻の機嫌をとりたかったため、そのコースに参加することにしました。

The instructor was an elderly man who was so short that he had to stand on a box to see over the "etsubin", a Japanese term for a cast iron kettle used for boiling water.

講師の人は年配の男性でしたが、彼はとても背が低かったため箱の上に立って、湯を沸かすための日本の鉄製のやかんである"鉄瓶"越しで見渡さなければなりませんでした。

This one in front of him was huge, nearly a yard across and heated from hot stones pulled from the nearby springs.

彼の前にあるそれは大きく、約1ヤードの大きさで、近くの温泉から取り出された熱い石で熱せられました。

To our disgust, he threw living frogs into the open kettle, where they crashed into the water with a great *hiss* and sizzle.

不快なことに、彼は生きているカエルを蓋がされていないやかんに入れ、その途端シューシューという大きな音が鳴りました。

Frogs have always been one of my favorite animals, and I treat them with a kind of reverence they may not even deserve.

カエルは私の好きな動物の一つで、彼らにふさわしいものではないかもしれませんが、私は彼らにある種の尊敬の念をもって接していました。

But I felt that I had to protest this cruel behavior.

しかし、私はその残酷な行動に抗うべきだと思いました。

I stepped forward and shouted at him like a drunken sailor, loud and obnoxiously so that he would surely get my message.

私は前に出て、彼に聞こえるように、酔っぱらった水兵のように声高にかつ口汚く彼に向かって叫びました。

"Hey man, what do you think you are doing!?

おい！何をやっているのかわかっているのですか！？

At least kill those frogs in a humane way.

少なくとも人道的な方法でそれらのカエルを殺すべきです。

Don't just toss them into boiling water like their lives are of so little value!"

彼らの命を尊重せずに、沸いている水に投げ入れるべきではないです！"

My wife pulled me aside and explained to me that one of the rules of this culture was never to disagree with your elders in a public setting, such as a meeting or a group course like the one we were partaking in.

妻は私を脇に引っ張り、日本文化では会議や私たちが参加しているようなグループコースなどの公の場で、年上の人に逆らってはいけないのだと私に説明しました。

She told me that I was doing the instructor a grave disservice and that I was causing him to "lose face", something they call "mentsu wo ushinau".

彼女は、その講師にとってはひどい仕打ちであり、私は彼の"顔をつぶす"つまり彼の"面子を失わせる"ことをしてしまったと言いました。

I looked at the little old man and saw him scowling at me, his face turning a deep purple under his kasa.

私がその背の低い男を見ると、彼は怖い顔をしてこちらを見ており、また彼の顔は笠の下で濃い紫色に変わっていました。

But this did not matter to me at the time.

しかし、その時私は気にしませんでした。

I was so taken aback by his treatment of the frogs that I was blinded by rage; all custom and delicacy was thrown to the wind.

私は、彼のそのカエルの扱いに驚き、また怒りで礼儀や気遣いを忘れ周囲が見えなくなっていました。

I pointed my finger at him and explained that animal cruelty was something I simply could not let go.

私は彼の方へ指を差し、動物虐待は許されないことだと説明しました。

"End this show right now! This…this…spectacle!"

"この見世物を終わらせてくれ！この…この…ショーを！"

Unexpectedly, he came forward and jabbed a finger into my chest and told me that "we are still in Japanese territory" or something of the like.

思いもよらず、彼は前に出て指で私の胸を突き"私たちはまだ日本にいる"といったようなこと言いました。

My wife then whispered into my ear that he had challenged me; I guessed he wanted me to show the audience a real alternative to the process he adhered to.

妻は私の耳元で、彼は私を挑発していると囁き、私は、彼は私に周りの人々に彼のその行為に替わるものを見せて欲しいのではないかと思いました。

I saw him standing there, now with a smug smile spreading across his face, motioning me towards the box where he had been presiding over the boiling cauldron.

彼はそこに立ち、顔には得意げな笑みを浮かべ、沸騰している大釜越しで講義をしていたその箱に来るよう私に合図をしました。

He gestured again and suddenly I became unsure of myself.

彼は再び同じ合図をしましたが、私は突然自信を持てなくなりました。

I had never cooked frogs in my life.

私は今までカエルを料理したことがありません。

But I decided to show some courage and approached the wooden platform.

しかし、私はいくらかの勇気を見せることを決め、木製の演台へと近づいていきました。

I would end this spectacle on my own terms.

私は私自身でこのショーを終わらせることでしょう。

The people around us, the tourists and growing crowd of locals alike, applauded, curiosity plainly written on their faces.

私たちの周囲にいた観光客や地元の人々は、拍手を送り、彼らの顔は好奇心あふれる顔でした。

When I stepped up onto the box and looked out onto the crowd, I was quite at a loss about what to do.

私がその箱の上に上がって群集を見た時、何をするべきなのか困ってしまいました。

I didn't have the heart to kill these frogs, no matter the method.

どのような手段を使ったとしても、私はこれらのカエルを殺す気などありませんでした。

So in the end, I decided that the best course of action was just to take the bag with the frogs away.

結局、とるべき行動はカエルを鞄に入れて持ち去ることだと思いました。

That way, they could live a happy life amongst the puddles and rotten drainage.

そうすれば、カエルは水たまりや腐食した排水管で幸せな日々を送るでしょう

At least I would end this cruel charade!

少なくとも、私はこの残酷なゲームを終わらせるでしょう！

I started to gather all the frogs and place them tenderly in the bag, for I did not want to crush any of them in my haste.

私は全てのカエルを集め始め、傷つけないようにそっと鞄の中に入れました。

I was about to make a break for it, when I was suddenly pushed from behind.

突然後ろから押された時、危うくカエルを傷つけることころでした。

I fell forward and before I knew it, my entire being was awash in blinding pain.

私は、気づく前に前方に倒れ、全身がひどい痛みであふれていました。

Heat enveloped me; I felt it sear my bones.

私の体は熱さで覆われ、骨は焼け焦がれたような感覚でした。

I passed out.

そして、私は気絶しました。

When I came to, I was in the hospital that I mentioned at the beginning of this tale.

意識が戻った時、このお話の冒頭で述べたように私は病院の中にいました。

The sterile surroundings confused me; I was awash in hard, white light.

無菌環境に戸惑い、私は白い光にさらされていました。

I quickly noticed that my legs and feet were wrapped entirely in bandages.

すぐに、私の両足全体が包帯で巻かれていることに気づきました。

I looked at my arms: the surface of my skin looked like dirty, pinkish crushed stone.

自分の腕を見ると、皮膚は汚いように見え、石でぶつけたかのようにピンクがかっていました。

Later, the Japanese doctor teasingly scolded me.

後に、日本人の医者はからかうように私を叱りました。

"Mister, this is what you get for causing someone to lose face.

"ご主人、他人の面子をつぶすとこうなるのです。

You have only been boiled alive."

あなたは生きたまま煮られただけです。"

50. The Legend of princess Kaguya

かぐや姫物語

The legend of princess Kaguya (Kaguya-hime no Monogatari) is one of the oldest passed on folk tales in Japan.

かぐや姫物語は、日本で最も古い民話です。

It's about princess Kaguya who is originally from the moon-kingdom, and who descended to earth to live as a human, daughter of a poor couple.

月の国からきたかぐやというお姫様が、

地球に降りたち、貧しい夫婦の娘となって人間とともに生活をする、というお話です。

One day an old man who collects bamboo goes into a woods to cut bamboo.

ある日、老人が竹を集めに森の中へ入ってきました。すると、なにやら金色に輝く竹の棒が1つあります。

One bamboo-stick is shining golden and as he cuts the bamboo stick, he finds a small girl inside the stick.

老人がその竹を切ると、なんとその中に小さな女の子がいるのを発見したのです。

He took the small girl home where he and his wife are raising the girl with love and care. They name the girl Kaguya Hime, the shining princess.

老人はその女の子を家へ連れて帰り、妻とともに愛情を込めて育てました。光り輝く姫という意味をこめ、かぐや姫と名づけました。

Within a few years she becomes a beautiful young woman. Ever since the Kaguya princess has lived with the couple, they were able to find some small amounts of gold, and thereby escaped complete poverty.

数年後、かぐや姫はとても美しい娘に育ちました。かぐや姫がこの夫婦と暮らし始めてから、金が少量手に入るようになり、貧しさからは完全に抜け出していました。

Since Kaguya became a woman, her beauty had become known in the whole province and many men wanted to win her over.

かぐや姫が大人の女性になると、彼女の美しさのうわさは地域中に広がり、たくさんの男性が彼女をお嫁にしたい、と望むようになります。

She rejected one after another and send them home.

けれどもかぐや姫は、次から次へと求婚に来る男たちを断り続け、家に帰らせました。

After a while only five man were left. To test their seriousness Kaguya gave them an impossible task.

やがて残ったのは、5人の男性だけでした。彼らの真剣さを確かめるために、かぐや姫はとても難しい試練を与えます。

Most of the admirers tried shortcuts, and no man succeeded. Some men even died in the effort.

ほとんどの求婚者は、試験に通れるよう近道をしようとするのですが、だれも成功する者はいません。なかには、努力のかいもなく死んでしまった者もいました。

After the failure of all men, the emperor himself became curious, and tried to court her himself.

多くの男たちが失敗したのちに、帝は興味を持ちはじめ、かぐや姫を嫁に迎えいれようと試みます。

But eventually Kaguya even rejected the emperor.

けれども、かぐや姫は帝からの求婚も断ります。

One night she starred at the moon and revealed sadly to her parents that she wanted to to return to the moon-kingdom.

ある夜、姫は悲しそうに月を見つめながら、月の国へ帰らなければならないことを両親に告げます。

Although the imperial troops tried to prevent her from leaving, on a full moon night she thanked her parents for the love they gave her and then was carried away by coach back to the moon.

かぐや姫は愛情を注いでくれた両親に感謝を伝え、朝廷の兵隊たちが姫の旅立ちを防ごうといているそばで、牛車に乗って月の国へ飛び立っていったのでした。

Christian Tamaka Pedersen is the founder of the Yokahama English Japanese Language & Teachers Club. To support him or to make suggestions you can contact him at:
https://www.patreon.com/japanesebooks

CPSIA information can be obtained
at www.ICGtesting.com
Printed in the USA
BVHW040920220920
589359BV00012B/166